D0848319

*Parish Churches of England
in Colour*

Parish Churches of England

in Colour

Mervyn Blatch

Foreword by Alec Clifton-Taylor

BLANDFORD PRESS
London

To Eileen

First published in 1974
by Blandford Press Ltd,
167 High Holborn, London WC1V 6PH
© Blandford Press 1974
ISBN 0 7137 0630 9

Printed in Great Britain by Tinling (1973) Ltd, Liverpool
Colour printed by Colour Reproductions, Billericay

CONTENTS

FOREWORD

When I was invited to write a foreword for this book I accepted with pleasure, for Mr Blatch is an old friend in whose company I have travelled a great many miles, seeking out churches of special interest to us both.

His concern has always been primarily as a photographer, and to what good effect may now be judged. There are already many books on the English parish churches – I have recently been rash enough to add another to their number myself – but up till now an anthology of colour photographs, in which every single county is represented, and obtainable moreover at a very reasonable price, has never been available.

In the text Mr Blatch has written of the churches as he has found them and shows a deep affection for his subject, but it is for his splendid photographs that this book is likely to be especially enjoyed and treasured.

Many more pictures were taken than are here presented, for nothing but the highest standards would satisfy him, and hours of thought have been devoted to such matters as achieving a proper balance between the styles, a nice contrast between the materials, a neat setting of the familiar against the unfamiliar. The outcome is a book with a very personal viewpoint, which is one more reason why I am so happy to introduce it.

Alec Clifton-Taylor

ACKNOWLEDGEMENTS

There are certain people without whom some books would never have been written.

First and foremost in the case of this book, I must place Lawrence E. Jones, the indefatigable honorary lecturer for the Historic Churches Preservation Trust, the body which does more than any other to arouse interest in and help to maintain our precious heritage of old churches. Lawrence Jones has given hours of his time, advising me, correcting and making suggestions from his unrivalled knowledge of the subject. This is quite apart from the numerous excursions I have made in his company. I cannot thank him sufficiently for all his encouragement and help.

A very special word of thanks must go to Alec Clifton-Taylor, who has kindly written the foreword. His classic work, *The Pattern of English Building*, has been the inspiration to me for my particular approach and no one has done more to stimulate my interest and to educate me in churches. We must have visited together a large number.

I must also express my great debt to the 'Buildings of England' series of books, edited by Sir Nikolaus Pevsner. The gratitude that all who visit churches must feel towards him and his co-authors can never be fully measured. For me, these books have been the source of countless discoveries and a great deal of information, and I rarely go on a visit to churches without the appropriate volume. I have tried to point the way, but for those who wish to explore a county thoroughly there is no substitute for the 'Pevsner' covering that particular county.

My indebtedness to the foregoing authors must be obvious and in several places I have included quotations from their books where it would be inappropriate to improve on what is already so well expressed. Beyond obvious quotation there must be an invisible indebtedness for concepts and approaches to the subject and I trust that I have not un-wittingly neglected adequate acknowledgement. In spite of the help from my expert colleagues, and the assistance of the many church guides I have consulted, I must, of course, accept full responsibility for the text matter which follows.

My family have played a big part. My wife has spent much time in reading and spotting infelicities of phrase, when my sometimes wayward mode of expression has offended her stricter grammatical standards. My daughter has spent many hours typing and I am most grateful to them both.

Finally, I would thank my publishers for their consideration and help. I appreciate, too, their indulgence on extended deadlines. One of the many pleasures of writing this book has been the agreeable and fruitful discussions with the editors, notably John Chesshyre and Penelope Davies, at each stage of the work.

INTRODUCTION:
THE VARIED FACE OF OLD
ENGLISH CHURCHES

Whatever the season, whatever the weather, the parish churches of England are there, waiting to be visited, perhaps for one to say a prayer or just to look at and enjoy. Of the nearly seventeen thousand parishes in the country, no less than ten thousand of the places of worship are mediaeval or of mediaeval origin. Wherever one may be, there is sure to be an old church well worth a visit not far away.

One can never hope to see them all, however, and it is doubtful whether any living person has achieved this distinction. If one averaged two a week, it would take a hundred years just to get around the mediaeval ones.

Some visitors to these churches may prefer to allow the beauty of the building to flow over them like a piece of music, without regard to any particular aspect. Others may feel the need to have some thread running through their church-visiting; perhaps to study the different styles of architecture, to see how the church has gradually evolved from modest beginnings; or to concentrate upon particular features such as screens or fonts; yet others may have an interest in the monuments and the story they tell of the lives of our ancestors and the social conditions in which they lived. There must also be many who are mainly concerned with the building as a place of worship, drawing them nearer to God.

One approach, which will be followed in this book, is to examine the effect of economic and social conditions, together with the availability of building materials and means of transport, on the form and visual impact of the buildings. Why, for instance, in areas like the East Riding of Yorkshire and East Anglia, not richly blessed with good building stone, are there so many noble parish churches which often tax local resources to the limit to maintain? Why is it that, so frequently, flatter landscapes like those of East Anglia, Lincolnshire and Northamptonshire are compensated by fine churches, whereas counties with more spectacular scenery like Derbyshire or Dorset are less well endowed in this respect? Why is the prosperous south-east a relatively modest field for mediaeval churches and yet a happy hunting-ground for the Victorian ecclesiologist? As one travels around, one becomes aware of these and many other differences.

Some districts are spire districts; others have towers only. Some areas are rich in woodwork; others in stonework. Some counties have large churches, even in country surroundings; others have small buildings, even in more populous centres. But, nearly everywhere, the stately town places of worship lie not far removed from humble village houses of God, so that the one acts as a foil to the other. No two are exactly alike, and most have some special feature of particular note or beauty.

In order to set the scene, it is necessary to define the regions and the period of time this book covers. One could take regions on a geological basis, according to the building material available, or on a social and economic basis, according to their relative prosperity when the churches were built. We could go back to the fourth century, when probably the earliest church in England was erected to the south-east of the Roman forum at Silchester, and bring the story up to the present day.

It has, however, seemed that a simple geological/geographical division would be the most helpful and that the Middle Ages – which, for this purpose, I have assumed to be the five hundred years from 1040 to 1540 – provide the greatest regional individuality, although reference to what went before will be included. Nevertheless, a brief historical survey covering the whole period of church building will put matters into perspective, and this will be the subject of the opening chapter.

English people have strong county loyalties and individual preferences. In order, therefore, to be as objective as possible, the illustrations are spread over the whole country, not necessarily showing the most famous buildings, but those which are typical and many which are little known.

Finally, a word as to the counties themselves. For administrative convenience the old boundaries, based on historical, geographical and other factors, have been radically altered. The new divisions may logically be justified but take no account of psychological loyalties. They ignore age-old considerations which go deep into our past and it will, in my view, be long before they are accepted in our hearts as well as by our heads. I have, therefore, adhered to the boundaries existing prior to the recent Government changes, with the exception of leaving Middlesex as it was before 1965 (when it was gobbled up by London, Hertfordshire and Surrey), but including with Huntingdonshire, the Soke of Peterborough.

1 HISTORY OF CHURCH BUILDING

The earliest Christian church in England was probably the building erected about 350 yards to the south-east of the Roman forum at Silchester, in Hampshire. It was very small – the nave measured thirty feet by ten feet – and was made in the form of a basilica, or hall of justice, with an apse at the west end. The sites of churches, however, often go back much further. Many a Bronze Age ring-barrow was taken over by Christians to bury their dead, and circular churchyards, such as Lamport in Northamptonshire and Oxted in Surrey, may well denote a pre-Christian burial site, or even temple.

It is doubtful, however, whether construction really made headway until St Augustine landed in Kent in AD 597. His mission seems to have been extraordinarily successful and it is said that, at the confluence of the rivers Swale and Medway, he baptized ten thousand people on Christmas Day that year. There are still remains of ten churches built by the saint and his followers in Kent during the seventh century. These include the church of St Martin, Canterbury, which may even have existed before St Augustine landed, for Bede records that Bertha, the Christian Queen of Kent, worshipped there before the missionary's arrival. Like Ethelburga, the Kentish wife of Edwin the Northumbrian King, thirty years later, the queens prepared the way for the conversions of the kings.

In the North, a parallel impetus to building was the arrival in Northumbria in AD 674 of Benedict Biscop, an Anglian of noble birth. Biscop, who had been a monk in France, brought over with him stonemasons from Gaul so that when he founded his monasteries at Monkwearmouth and Jarrow they were built of stone. This was a great step forward in the development of English building and original parts of these two churches still remain. Not far away at Escomb (pl. 66), also in County Durham, there is another contemporary church which is almost completely preserved so that it is possible to study the proportions of these early houses of God. They are noticeably tall and narrow, with a chancel of minute size and a pinched arch leading into it. Windows are small with deep splays and the masonry is remarkably good for such an early date. This group of northern churches which also includes parts of Corbridge in Northumberland (pl. 68), differs markedly from the Kentish group in having square and not rounded east ends (apses) and in reflecting Celtic rather than Roman traditions. From the blending of these two streams, the characteristic English church was to emerge.

On a grander scale was the Anglo-Saxon church at Brixworth in Northamptonshire, described by Sir Alfred Clapham as 'perhaps the most imposing architectural memorial of the seventh century surviving north of the Alps'. What we see today – extensive as it is – is only part of the original church, which has been shorn of its aisles. There is no doubt, however, that with an exterior length of 140 feet and a breadth across the nave of thirty feet, it is a fine example of the early Anglo-Saxons' building ability.

Despite this growth of Christianity, the balance between civilization and barbarism was very finely poised and before the end of the eighth century men from the north – this time from Scandinavia – were invading England, harrying and pillaging wherever they went. Famous centres of learning, like Lindisfarne Abbey in Northumberland, were burnt to the ground, their treasures looted and their monks slaughtered. Not until Alfred the Great succeeded in stemming the tide of Viking penetration, could church-building be resumed. Alfred himself translated the works of Bede from Latin to Anglo-Saxon. From the reign of Edgar (959–75), churches were erected all over the country, mostly of wood but many of stone, and it is calculated that more than 250 of our existing buildings are Anglo-Saxon or show Anglo-Saxon features. It is difficult to single out any one area, but Lincolnshire and Northamptonshire are especially rich in work of this period.

In the eleventh century, however, civilizing influences were again brought to a halt by an invader. Although King Canute provided good and conciliatory government, he did not live long enough to establish a line of kings which could stand up to yet another invader, this time from Normandy. So, after a successful campaign, William, Duke of Normandy, became William I of England.

At first, these French Vikings were more concerned with erecting castles to maintain control of their newly conquered territory than with building churches.

When the Normans did get around to it, the sparsity of the population precluded building on the grand scale, except in a few places like Melbourne in Derbyshire and Walsoken in Norfolk, and their cautious finance led to construction proceeding at a slow pace. They did, on the other hand, bring order and energy to their building, in contrast to the somewhat haphazard ways of their predecessors. In many respects they were not as good masons as the Anglo-Saxons, and their craftsmanship was often poor. The continued use of the round arch made anything ambitious in the way of vaulting very hazardous, and when it was attempted towers frequently fell, causing much damage. The Normans imposed a uniform and heavy style with dark and forbidding interiors. Piers were short, circumscribed by the semicircular arch and no attempt at decoration was made, beyond a single chamfer or moulding on the arch, or orange or red painting. Capitals were square in shape as were the bases of the piers. Nowhere can the mark of a heavy-handed and insensitive conqueror be felt more strongly than in the parish church of Blyth in Nottinghamshire, although here the piers have square cores and shafts. Later, the Norman style softened and blossomed forth into vigorous decoration of fonts, doorways, arches and capitals.

Norman fonts, of which many remain, were capacious in accordance with the contemporary custom of baptism by immersion. Regional characteristics were first displayed by these fonts, in contrast to the more uniform style of the churches built throughout the period. Among the different types of font are:

Lead fonts. These were once common, but only about thirty now remain. Many ended up as bullets for Cromwellian and, one suspects, Royalist muskets. They are to be found in various parts of the country and some of the more notable ones will be mentioned in the regional chapters.

Aylesbury fonts. As the name indicates, this is a local type found in and around Aylesbury, Buckinghamshire. Beautifully proportioned, they have a base made of decorated half-circles with deep indentations between. Upon these rests a narrow band with zigzag ornamentation, above which the font opens out with fluting to a top encircled with a delicate foliage band.

Cornish fonts. Another local type with two subdivisions. These are:

(a) A cup-bowl, elaborately carved and with central supporting stem. Four angle shafts rising outside the bowl are capped with sculptured heads, as at Roche.

(b) A Norman capital with a single, but more massive, central support. The sides in the shape of roundels are carved with rosettes and other decorations. Between each side, at the top, is a sculptured head.

Herefordshire fonts. Yet another local type Goblet-shaped, they are carved with a mass of symbolic designs, some drawn from Irish motifs. It seems possible that the two most famous, Eardisley and Castle Frome, together with the south doorway at Kilpeck (pl. 81) emanated from a school of stone-carving probably located at Leominster, where there was a Benedictine abbey. The sculpture is wonderfully executed, notably the two warriors with Phrygian caps on the bowl at Eardisley.

Black Tournai marble fonts. Although not so local, four of the remaining eight of this type are in Hampshire, in churches not far from the coast. These fonts were mass-produced at Tournai, Belgium, where the blue-black limestone of which they were made was quarried. They are square in shape with a recessed bowl, supported on a central post with four corner posts.

Towards the end of the Norman period (1066 to nearly the end of the twelfth century) carving on the tympana (the spaces in the heads of doorway arches) became common. Malmesbury, Wiltshire, has a notable Norman porch which shows the apostles with an angel flying horizontally above. Doors became deeply recessed with a riot of carving on the several orders of arches. Iffley in Oxfordshire is an excellent example of this type. Nave arcades became lighter and less static, as at St Peter, Northampton.

The simple, rugged strength of Norman buildings had thus gradually changed into a lighter, less heavy style. Many of the village churches are very charming, particularly Elkstone in Gloucestershire, Barfreston in Kent and, best of all, Kilpeck in Herefordshire (pl. 81).

But as long as the round arch was retained there was no scope for further advance in architectural style. In England, some experiments in style were made in 1128–33 in the nave of Durham Cathedral where, for the first time, the transverse arches were pointed. But it was not until towards the third quarter of the twelfth century, after a long transitional period, that Early English, the first of the Gothic styles, began to take over, and church architecture changed from the static equilibrium of the Norman style to something more dynamic.

Early English architecture is basically austere, reflecting to some extent the self-denying attitude of the Cistercian monastic order, founded by St Bernard in France in 1098. There is little doubt that the great break-through from the round Norman to the pointed Gothic style was powerfully influenced by this order and the way they built their religious houses. The earliest Cistercian house in England, Waverley in Surrey, was founded in 1128, but it took some time for the new architectural ideas to permeate through to the parish churches, although when churches were extended or rebuilt in the Early English style they were usually connected with a monastery.

During the Transitional period, extending from the middle of the twelfth century, Norman and Early English methods tended to become intermingled but, in essence, the Early English style is a thirteenth-century fashion. It was mainly directed towards increasing height and space within a church by lightening the construction; walls became thinner and were pierced to give more window space. The style is distinguished by narrow pointed windows, called 'lancets', in groups of two, three, occasionally five, and very rarely seven. Ockham in Surrey and Blakeney in Norfolk have good windows of this type. Tracery had not been evolved and there was little decoration, the whole emphasis being on verticality to carry the congregation's thoughts heavenwards. Towers, still infrequent, were usually plain and unbuttressed, although buttresses were used to compensate for the thinner walls and to carry the stress of the roof. A vaulted roof was sometimes supported by the graceful flying type of buttress. Aisles were added, usually on the north side, by building outwards, and then, when the aisle was covered, punching through the nave walls to provide an arcade. Often, too, round apses were removed in order to lengthen the chancel.

Roofs were gabled and never flat, except when lean-to over aisles. Vaulting was rare, except under towers and occasionally in porches, as at Barnack in the Soke of Peterborough. Piers were usually circular but sometimes octagonal and occasionally shafted. Their bases often had deeply cut mouldings, known as water-holding mouldings (Ivychurch, Kent, has these), and capitals were normally moulded with deeply undercut rounds and hollows, although occasionally ornamented with stiff-leaf capitals. These latter are one of the most enjoyable features of the style and perhaps none more so than those at Eaton Bray in Bedfordshire, West Walton in Norfolk and East Hendred in Berkshire. The abacus was almost always round. For general decoration, the only other motif used was the carved pyramidal or dog-tooth form.

Thirteenth-century work is common in the south-east and Essex, but it is seen at its best where limestone was available, and in the north-east. It is infrequent in the south-west, Lancashire, Cheshire and East Anglia. Many churches in the Midlands retain their thirteenth-century arcades despite the fact that the aisles were widened later. In cathedrals and large churches Purbeck marble was widely used for decorative shafting. Indeed, the Early English style, in all its severity and, perhaps, coldness, is seen in the grandeur of Salisbury Cathedral, built almost wholly in this style. There is, nevertheless, a purity and spirituality about the style which is intensely satisfying. And Pevsner, describing one of the finest Early English parish churches, Felmersham in Bedfordshire (pl. 15), refers to this period of church-building as 'the noblest age of mediaeval churches'.

Towards the close of the thirteenth century, the 'ascetic force', to quote F. H. Crossley, declined, and architecture became more human. There was less emphasis on height and more on breadth, so that churches became less austere. It was the age of chivalry and a time when women were held in high esteem, a fact reflected in the importance given to the Virgin Mary. Window tracery became geometrical, then reticulated, and finally, flowing and intricate. There was much regional variety and Kentish tracery is still a common term of description.

Arches continued to be pointed, but less sharply. Piers were usually octagonal, although sometimes four or eight half-shafts are attached to a central square pier. Fillets were used at the end of the thirteenth and in the first half of the fourteenth century. Bases were a pair or triplet of rolls while the abacus was often octagonal. Capitals might still be entirely moulded, but when depicting foliage (oak, ivy, maple and vine), a more natural style was used. The main form of ornamentation was the ball-flower, a globular flower with three incurved petals.

Perhaps in no other period do we find greater regional individuality, and it is therefore especially pertinent to our subject. It was as though masons and craftsmen felt at liberty to express themselves in the way they believed would best enhance God's glory, and the liberation of the human spirit resulted in buildings where God's presence could be more intimately experienced than in the grander but more worldly style that followed. The craftsman was, moreover, still subordinate to the mason so that buildings were not considered just as a framework for the skills of the glazier and the woodcarver. The large churches of East Anglia indicate the great wealth derived from sheep-rearing in the fen country, whence wool was exported to the Continent, while weaving brought prosperity to the east Midlands, as the great stone spires of Northamptonshire, Rutland and the Kesteven area of Lincolnshire show.

It is convenient to define the period of this new Gothic style, normally called Decorated, as spanning the reigns of the first three Edwards (1272–1377). But the death-knell of this style was sounded earlier than 1377 by the most appalling of national catastrophes, the Black Death. This severe outbreak of bubonic plague raged throughout 1348–49 and was responsible for the death of one-third of the population of England and the disappearance of three thousand villages. The life went out of the Decorated style and it was replaced by something altogether different.

Up to that time, Gothic styles followed a parallel course in England and in France, but now the ways parted. In France, the Decorated was taken to extreme lengths in the Flamboyant style, while this side of the Channel the peculiarly English style, Perpendicular, evolved. The first suggestion of this style had appeared even before the Black Death, owing to an unusual combination of circumstances, in the rebuilding of the east end of Gloucester Cathedral. This foundation had become rich from the offerings of pilgrims to the shrine of Edward ii. Abbot Thoky had raised the status of this unworthy king to that of a martyr by obtaining his murdered body from Berkeley Castle and building the shrine. At the same time, there was an advanced school of Severn masons who took the opportunity to experiment with the new style. But for these conditions, the Perpendicular form of architecture might never have received general acceptance in this country.

But, as a result of the Black Death, there was an acute lack of skilled masons and craftsmen as well as a marked economic decline and there was little building until the last quarter of the fourteenth century. When it was resumed, parish church construction took premier place, for the scourge had depleted the monasteries and, later, the Wars of the Roses were to impoverish many members of the aristocracy. It was the increasingly wealthy merchants who became the principal patrons of the new buildings that were being erected, perhaps with an eye to ensuring their position in the next world.

As the name 'Perpendicular' implies, there was emphasis on the upward line. Mullions were carried right up to the head of the window, but the style could, in many cases, be called 'horizontal', for transoms were sometimes carried right across. Arches tended to be more obtuse and often four-centred, and, in Tudor times, even straight-headed. Greater importance was given to interiors than exteriors, and the aim was to produce an aisleless hall, in which a wooden screen stretching right across replaced the chancel arch to give an effect that has been aptly called 'tranquil spaciousness'.

Mouldings were mainly the casement and double ogee. As the arch became blunter piers were more pronounced and usually octagonal with half-shafts and mouldings. Bases were normally polygonal with a high plinth. Abaci were more often chamfered on their upper edge instead of rounded. Small leaves or flowers of square form in a hollow were used as ornament, as was brattishing (a cresting of upright leaves). Light stone panelling was also often used for decorative purposes.

A double series of closely set windows in nave and clerestory led to the term 'glasshouse' sometimes being applied to the magnificent churches which arose in the wealthier parts of the land – the so-called 'wool' areas of Lincolnshire, East Anglia, the East Riding of Yorkshire, Gloucestershire and Somerset.

This Perpendicular form of construction made less demands on the skill of the mason, who was in short supply after the Black Death anyway, and he tended to subordinate his efforts to the craftsman; the interiors became a platform for the virtuosity of the glazier, the woodworker and the sculptor. The mason, however, achieved great feats with glorious towers and beautiful stone fan-vaulting. This was the age of tower-building and it was found that the new and splendid towers which were going up did not need a spire to complete them. Guttering, too, had been introduced, so that it was no longer necessary to rely upon the steep pitch of the roof to take away rain-water, consequently roofs became flatter. Parapets to hide a flat roof, therefore, became important and these were frequently battlemented. Between 1350 and 1535, which roughly corresponds with the span of Perpendicular architecture, several thousand towers were built and many earlier churches were enlarged or rebuilt. No other country can offer so many examples of splendid tower construction as England.

In studying regional differences, towers and spires will loom large.

These features are the most prominent distinguishing marks of local pride and resource, and show the greatest variety. It therefore seems appropriate to include a chapter on these features alone. Suffice it to say here that Somerset is above all others for the variety and richness of its beautiful towers.

So lavish was the money set aside in the wealthy wool and cloth-weaving areas of England that many of the churches were rebuilt completely and are therefore of one style. In other areas, notably the Midlands, altering the church was a process of slow growth, so that all styles may be represented in the one building. In general, however, it must be stated that regional individualism was replaced by a certain uniformity which, splendid as it often was, could at times be repetitive.

The Reformation was succeeded by a lull in church construction. Of course, places of worship were erected in the latter years of Henry VIII's reign, such as the endearing little church at Esher, Surrey, but they are few and far between and, in the following reigns, parish-church building came almost to a complete standstill. Elizabethan houses are quite common, but Elizabethan churches are very rare. Few churches were built in the first half of the seventeenth century and it was not until after the Great Fire of London in 1666 that the need was felt for more churches. One of our greatest architects, Sir Christopher Wren, was then responsible for much of the rebuilding of London. He introduced Baroque motifs to the City of London and there was a return to Classical forms, but in a somewhat tentative manner. It was not until the eighteenth century that Wren's successors, Nicholas Hawksmoor and Thomas Archer, produced their own splendid brand of Baroque, of which St Paul's Church, Deptford, is the best example. The Georgian years were a period of elegance and dignity, and these qualities, combined with simple and decorous furnishings designed for Protestant worship, produced a rich harvest of delightful churches. Blandford, Dorset; Avington and Wolverton, Hampshire; St Chad, Shrewsbury; Great Witley, Worcestershire; Gayhurst, Buckinghamshire; Glynde, Sussex, are but a few. Nostalgic features are the box-pews and three-decker pulpits, as at Whitby on the Yorkshire coast and Minstead, Hampshire.

It would be misleading to try and pick out regional features in these post-Reformation churches. The appearance of the architect with a national practice, as opposed to the local mason with a regional reputation, caused local styles to lose their individuality and although there were many competent local architects, like the Bastard brothers at Blandford, Dorset, it would be stretching facts to say that they evolved a local pattern. Nevertheless, the heritage of eighteenth-century churches, if not perhaps so outstanding as that of Georgian domestic architecture, is a precious one.

Even in Wren's time Gothic as well as Classical churches were being erected; St Mary Aldermary and the tower and spire of St Dunstan-in-the-East in the City of London, designed by him, are Gothic buildings. This became more pronounced as time went on until, in the nineteenth century, the Gothic Revival took over from Classical forms. The early nineteenth-century churches were somewhat timid essays in the Decorated style and the so-called Commissioners' churches, built to fill a gap after the Napoleonic Wars, were erected on the cheap.

Thereafter, the building of churches fell into the hands of architects who, although professional and skilled, were unduly influenced by the views on church ceremonial held by the Camden Society and the Tractarian Movement; these insisted that the only proper place in which to worship was a Gothic building, preferably in the Middle Pointed or Decorated style, ignoring the fact that one could not bring back to a totally different age the mediaeval spirit which inspired the great Gothic churches. In addition, the Camden Society laid down that box-pews should be removed, plaster and whitewash must be scraped away, thus destroying many wall-paintings which still remained under their Reformation coat of lime-wash, and that the sanctuary must be adorned with stained glass and colour. They favoured the introduction of large choirs of men and boys into the chancel, so that it became necessary to crowd that part with rows of pitch-pine pews. All this, as F. H. Crossley points out, was a process of 'Germanizing' Victorian England.

The experiments of nineteenth-century architects took many forms and it would be unjust to suppose that they were all bad. On the contrary, many of the churches built to meet the needs of a rapidly growing and pious people by the later Victorian architects, such as J. L. Pearson and G. F. Bodley, were outstanding buildings. These included Truro Cathedral and the impressive private church of the Duke of Newcastle at Clumber, Nottinghamshire. There are numerous Victorian churches and even village churches, notably in Surrey, which are works of merit; Victorian architects also saved buildings which were falling into ruin and their survey work in this field was admirable, but their theory that one could only worship properly in a Gothic building and their fondness for the mediaeval spires of the East Midlands could not hide the fact that they were chasing a shadow without bringing back the substance.

Today, in a groping and far less hide-bound manner, making the best use of modern materials, we attempt in our new churches to evolve a contemporary style instead of merely aping those of the past and, if some are better than others, there is an authenticity which was lacking in the previous century.

2 THE SHAPE OF ENGLAND

England is fortunate in the variety of its geological strata. This not only gives infinite diversity to the landscape but also to the buildings. The different effects obtained by using velvet, cotton and silk in the making of clothes are obvious. In the same way, the impact on buildings of the materials used – stone, timber, brick, slates, thatch and tiles – can be equally marked. Stone may range in colour from red to grey, with many intermediate shades, and its hardness or softness will determine how much of the original structure survives today.

The natural processes out of which these building materials were formed go back to unknown eras of prehistory, when time was measured in millions of years, not centuries. The youngest rocks in this country are at least a million years old and the most ancient ones used for building purposes go back 500 million years. In geological terms our span stretches from the Tertiary to the Ordovician periods.

Geology, and the resultant geography, determine not only the materials available for construction but also the wealth of the land and the navigability of rivers, all important factors in influencing the shape and size of our mediaeval churches. In the Middle Ages, when they were built, materials could not be moved readily from one side of the country to the other. Stone and timber were conveyed within a limited area, but the general difficulty of transport enhanced the local character of our places of worship. By using materials close at hand buildings can merge into their environment in a way which they often fail to do if constructed of materials brought from afar.

For our purpose it is convenient to divide England into separate parts: the first covering the south-east part of the country running from Norfolk to Hampshire; the second the middle part running from Yorkshire through the Midlands to Dorset; the third the sandstone area of the West Midlands and the fourth all the area lying north and west of these regions. Geologically speaking, the first three include the younger formations, up to 225 million years, and the fourth covers the other half, 225 to 500 million years, of the geological time span referred to above. In other words, England becomes progressively older the further one travels from Dover.

Norfolk to Hampshire. This slice of England contains alluvial and glacial deposits of the last million years which produced such physical features as the Fens, the Norfolk Broads and Romney Marsh. These areas are largely devoid of building stone and yet, as we shall see later, they contain fine churches. The zone as a whole, however, is not without building materials altogether and the Cretaceous period (70 to 135 million years ago) gave us the chalk, greensand and wealden formations which yield a limited quantity of material that can be used. Chalk gives rise to the characteristic landscape of the North and South Downs, the Chilterns and other upland areas in this sector and, apart from the flints which are found with it, is the source of a rather soft white building limestone often called 'clunch'. Although this stone does not stand up well to external hazards such as smoke or frost, it is used in many places, especially in Berkshire and Cambridgeshire. The extreme whiteness is evident in the view of Compton Beauchamp Church (pl. 17) which is largely built of this material.

The weald and the encircling sandy areas compose most of Surrey and Sussex between the Downs and southern Kent, a region noted more for its timber than its stone in the Middle Ages. Nevertheless, a variety of stone was quarried in these areas, particularly in the vicinity of Reigate, which was an important quarrying centre in the south-east. Quality differs and ranges from the rough and tough Kentish ragstone, used by the Romans to build London's walls, to the more gracious and amenable Bargate and Wealden sandstones. Wealden and Reigate stones can be cut, and the latter was used in the Tower of London and Westminster Abbey. Bargate stone, which can only be roughly coursed, is a distinctive feature of parts of Surrey around Godalming. Because of the iron in its composition, it produces beautiful warm brown and yellow shades which, to quote Alec Clifton-Taylor, 'are in tune with a landscape of exceptional charm'. One can see it to advantage in the little church of Wotton, near Dorking, nestling under the North Downs. Wealden stone offers a wider variety of tints and is a splendid accompaniment to the soaring grandeur of Lancing College Chapel. Among the sandstone repertoire is a light brown, gritty material called carstone in the west of Norfolk and in Bedfordshire, which turns darker on use, giving it the name 'gingerbread' stone.

Relatively young as these stones are, they are not the most recent in time. During the Middle Ages two limestones, Quarr Abbey and Binstead, formed during the Tertiary period (1 to 70 million years ago), were obtained from the Isle of Wight. These played an important part in the architecture of Hampshire and Sussex, notably at Winchester, but they have not been worked since the mediaeval period. Coralline Crag, a limestone formed at the same time, has been quarried in Suffolk, but is of very limited significance.

To complete the picture, it should be mentioned that in Norman times these stones were eked out with limestone brought over from Caen in Normandy. Another type of stone found on or just below the surface of downs and heaths in the south-east in isolated boulders, is sarsen or heathstone. A hard and siliceous sandstone, it was difficult to cut, but can be seen roughly coursed in the towers of some churches in the Woking area of west Surrey.

If, however, the counties from Norfolk to Hampshire were not over-flush with good building stone they were more fortunate in respect of economic wealth. In the fourteenth century Middlesex, including London, and Norfolk were the counties most highly assessed for taxes. Although Middlesex owed this doubtful honour to being in and around the seat of government, Norfolk drew its wealth from the rearing of sheep. The long-wooled breed which thrived in the Fens produced a fleece much in demand on the Continent, to which it was exported from King's Lynn. To this circumstance we are indebted for the superb marshland churches of which Walpole St Peter (pl. 38) might lay claim to be one of the finest village churches in England.

Great individual fortunes did not start to accumulate until the middle or end of the century. Until then weaving had been a home industry, boosted by the arrival of the Flemings, but gradually it came into the hands of men who would today be called capitalists. General prosperity had already produced some notable places of worship but, as T. D. Atkinson remarks, 'it was the ability to pay cash down which gave us the churches of Salle and Long Melford (pl. 33), and the roofs of Needham Market, Cawston (pl. 41) and March'. Norfolk and Suffolk remained the centres of the weaving industry, Kersey in Suffolk and Worstead in Norfolk giving their names to goods which were made all over the country. Aylsham in Norfolk was a centre of linen-weaving.

The neighbouring parts of Cambridgeshire and Essex shared in the benefits and also to some extent Hertfordshire, which additionally had a valuable malting industry. There existed, too, specialized activities like the growing of saffron for yellow dye at Saffron Walden and the cutlery industry of Thaxted. The prosperity brought by these activities is reflected in the impressive churches of the places involved.

South of the Thames, however, the position was different. It is hard to credit today, but Surrey was little regarded because of the poorness of its soil, and, though Sussex had an iron industry and sold timber for shipbuilding, these were relatively small and so brought little wealth. Kent, on the other hand, seems to have enjoyed a general prosperity from its position between London and the Continent and its good farming land.

Yorkshire to Dorset. This is a sector of complete contrast. Although this middle band of England is older than the south-east and falls within the Jurassic period (135 to 180 million years old), it has not yet reached what might be called geological middle age. Not only does it contain our finest building stone but it benefited in the Middle Ages from a high level of economic well-being, which rose to affluence in the East Riding, Cotswolds and Somerset. The combination of these two factors has left a legacy of noble churches stretching throughout much of the area.

Running for three hundred miles, like a great crescent through the sector, is the so-called limestone belt. From this came the stones for the lovely Cotswold villages, the great churches of southern Lincolnshire, Northamptonshire, Gloucestershire and Somerset and, with the aid of water transport, the East Riding of Yorkshire and the Fens. Many of these are built of oolitic limestone, the name given to a particular type of this stone where the individual grains resemble the hard roe of a herring.

There are many varieties of oolitic limestone, all with differing characteristics of colour and consistency. The finest, from the builder's point of view, is generally considered to be Portland, but there are others more beautiful, such as the golden Cotswold stones or the urbane Ketton stone used to such splendid effect at Cambridge. Almost every county has its well-known name – Dorset, Purbeck; Somerset, Bath and Doulting; Wiltshire, Chilmark; Northamptonshire, Barnack and Weldon; Rutland, Clipsham and Lincolnshire, Ancaster. In the Middle Ages the most famous and sought after of these stones was Barnack, sadly, now worked out. Portland and Ketton, conversely, were late starters and it is curious that the fourteenth-century church at Ketton (pl. 49) which has its own fine stone, was built of Barnack material. Portland did not come into general use until Sir Christopher Wren employed it in the reconstruction of St Paul's Cathedral and in his other City of London churches.

A further enhancement is the stone roofing 'slate' which adds so much to the enjoyment of Cotswold buildings. This slate, which is not slate in the true geological sense of the term, comes from the famous Stonesfield Quarry in Oxfordshire. The Collyweston Quarry in Northamptonshire is another famous source of roofing slate.

Running beside the great limestone belt, west and north-west of it with interruptions here and there, is what is called the lias. Although also a limestone, it is not nearly such a reliable stone as oolite and is not much used today. One of the most interesting of the liassic stones is Ham Hill, found in many churches in southern Somerset and adjacent parts of Dorset. Not particularly durable, it has, on the other hand, an attractive brown hue owing to the iron in its composition, and the lichens which grow readily on it provide a pleasing texture.

Further north, in the Midlands region, lias stretches from north Oxfordshire to Kesteven in Lincolnshire, and the various warm tints which come from its ferruginous nature enhance the churches in the area. A notable example of oolite and lias in strips is the orange-coloured, sixteenth-century church at Whiston, Northamptonshire (pl. 55). So-called blue lias, rather more grey than blue, used to be quarried in the Lyme Regis district of Dorset; churches built of this material also occur further north, in the Bridgwater, Taunton and Glastonbury areas of Somerset. One can see it in combination with brown oolite in the glorious tower of North Petherton (pl. 96).

West Midlands. The older parts of England fall into two divisions, a largely sandstone area covering most of the counties of Worcestershire, Warwickshire, Staffordshire and Cheshire together with adjacent parts of Shropshire, Derbyshire and Leicestershire, and with the exception of the Peak areas and the Derbyshire dales, the scenically much more dramatic counties lying north and south-west of these. The sandstone extends northwards into Lancashire and Cumberland, into central Yorkshire and south-east Durham and south-westwards towards Gloucestershire, north Somerset and Devonshire, giving many delightful red sandstone churches in the area from Taunton to Torquay and the famous red Devonshire cliffs running from Torquay to Sidmouth.

The sandstone of the West Midland counties referred to above comes from the Triassic and Permian systems, some 180 to 270 million years of age. Much of it lies well below the surface; in some parts of the Black Country and Potteries of Staffordshire it is overlaid by coal. Its colour varies, but the main impression is one of pink or yellow. Much of the area is agriculturally very rich, and here the sandstone produces a satisfying understanding between man and nature. Unfortunately most of it weathers badly and much architectural detail has been lost, while owing to constant refacings the agreeable patina one associates with old buildings is absent. It flakes and crumbles, and sometimes whole pinnacles fall off. The most resistant of the red sandstones is found at St Bees in Cumberland and at Hollington in Staffordshire; it was the latter which, after much research, was chosen for Coventry Cathedral.

A limestone of this Midland region, known as magnesian limestone, is found in a narrow strip running almost due north from Nottingham into the west of Yorkshire and finishing in County Durham. It is a stone of character which lends itself to fine cutting and many of the great Yorkshire churches are built of it. Against its undoubted qualities must be set the fact that in an industrial atmosphere it tends to turn a rather disagreeable grey and to develop unsightly white patches.

Another material from the sandstone repertoire came from the earlier Jurassic period, 135 to 180 million years ago. This was a light brown stratum quarried at one time near Whitby in Yorkshire and used to good effect at Whitby and Rievaulx abbeys.

One rather unusual limestone must be mentioned – tufaceous limestone. This is formed by spring water bubbling up through another limestone and precipitating calcium carbonate upon it; in time this hardens and assumes a sponge-like appearance with many holes in its surface. A harder form is called travertine. It is used in two or three churches in Worcestershire, the best-known of which is Shelsley Walsh, but another example is at Eastham (pl. 83) near Tenbury Wells.

North-west and south-west England. The most ancient rocks of the land also form the grandest scenery – the Lake District, the Pennines, the combes and tors of Devonshire and the windswept coasts of Cornwall. Some of the stones were formed by igneous rather than sedimentary action, and one of the characteristics of Cornwall and the adjoining areas of Devonshire is the abundant use made of hard, intractable granite.

Mountains and moors, however, make poor pasture and are not productive of wealth. Furthermore the counties nearest the border with Scotland were subject to frequent incursions, which retarded development. According to tax assessments in the fourteenth century these were among the poorest counties, and, with the possible exception of Durham, this is reflected in the relatively modest architecture, which has few of the graces that one finds further south. This does not, however, apply to Devonshire which shared in the wealth brought by the cloth industry and, as a result, has many notable churches. It possesses, among many stones, the striking new red sandstone as well as the rocks formed during the same geological period as the old, which derive the name of Devonian from the area. Cornwall, because of its remoteness and the employment of granite and slate-stone, has a more distinctive individuality than almost any other county, but its churches are charming rather than great.

The sedimentary stones of this sector come mainly from the Carboniferous formations (270 to 350 million years ago) which are very much part of the north. The colours are sombre but they fit the landscape. Consisting of the coal measures, millstone grit and carboniferous limestones, they form the backbone of England from Derbyshire to the Border. Their rough textures and huge blocks seem to typify the rugged, durable qualities of the north. Millstone grit, of which one of the best known stones is Darley Dale from Derbyshire, forms the wild moorlands around the Pennines, while the presence of the coal measures has caused a mainly rural area to become one of the most highly industrialized regions of the country. Carboniferous limestone is not much used outside the immediate area where it is found, but it is responsible for some of the most beautiful scenery in England, such as the dales of the West Riding of Yorkshire.

This geological system includes the old lead mines, but the lead used for roofs, fonts and the sheathing of wooden spires probably came from the mines of the Mendips in Somerset.

Finally there are the very oldest formations, ranging from the Devonian (350 to 400 millions years) to Ordovician (440 to 500 million years). The occurrence of the former in what might be called its 'home' area, has already been mentioned. The old red sandstone which is frequently encountered west of the River Severn and occurs widely in Herefordshire. Unlike the friable new red sandstones of the west Midlands, some of the Herefordshire stone is extremely resistant and it is to this quality that we owe the wonderfully crisp carving of the Norman church of Kilpeck (pl. 81). A limestone of this type is also found in Devonshire and can be seen in some of the churches around Newton Abbot.

Finally, to gather a few loose ends, stone from the Silurian period (400 to 440 million years) was used in the Lakeland church of Hawkshead in Lancashire (pl. 73). At the other end of the country is Serpentine, a rock of igneous origin, of which the Lizard Peninsula is largely composed. The church of Landewednack (pl. 104), which lies near Lizard Point and is the most southerly in England, is partly built of this stone. These are but two more of the extensive range of materials the mediaeval masons used for their building, which now form part of England's great legacy of old churches.

3 TOWERS AND SPIRES

The most casual traveller can hardly fail to respond to the influence of church towers and spires on the English scene. There is no feature which gives more character and individuality to our towns and villages; even London, when Canaletto painted it in the eighteenth century, had one of the most dramatic and exciting skylines of steeples in the world. And yet, apart from their function to house the bells – and, of course, the ringers – they do not serve any constructional or ceremonial purpose. They are not dependent upon the size of the congregation nor the rest of the structure for their form. They are, in fact, as T. D. Atkinson has pointed out, an architectural luxury.

In consequence of this, towers and spires are affected not only by the material, money and men available to build them but also by more intangible influences such as fashion and local pride. In addition, therefore, to being the most important external feature of a place of worship, they show the greatest regional variation. This chapter, however, will be more concerned with the development of the tower from the plain and unsophisticated towers of Saxon times, to the breathtaking products of the late Middle Ages, and the part played by spires in this development.

Anglo-Saxon. In Saxon times, towers may have had a functional purpose other than housing the bells. Round towers are very frequent in Norfolk, where there are over one hundred, and in Suffolk, which has more than forty. Although this shape of tower obviated the necessity of obtaining stone for the corners, it is more likely that they were built for strength and to accommodate the villagers if there was an attack by the Danes. They are all near the sea or rivers, and are Saxon in origin. Nor, when first built, was there an opening low down, access was gained by a ladder which was hauled up afterwards.

In addition to this possible use as a place of refuge, they may also have served in some cases as a dwelling-place for the parish priest or a custodian.

Apart from the round towers, about eighty towers remain in whole or in part from Saxon times. Generally rough-hewn with little in the way of decoration, they nevertheless have a rugged vigour which accords with the character of the age, for example, Clapham in Bedfordshire, St Peter-at-Gowts in Lincoln, Kirk Hammerton in the West Riding and Monkwearmouth in Durham. These are all of the campanile form, tall and narrow, and doubtless derived from Italy. The most famous is the thousand-year-old one at Earl's Barton in Northamptonshire which, somewhat exceptionally, has quite an elaborate decoration of pilaster strips and baluster openings.

Long-and-short work, consisting of upright stones placed alternately with flat stones, was often used at the corners.

The only covering for these towers was a low pyramidal cap, but at Sompting, in Sussex, there is a Saxon example – unique in this country – of what is called a Rhenish helm. The top of each of the four stone gables of the walls rise to a point so that the roof between the gables forms a diamond pattern. This was the nearest the Anglo-Saxons came to building a spire, and the next development in this direction, at Barnack in the Soke of Peterborough, did not come until after the beginning of the thirteenth century.

Norman. In Norman times the most usual position of the tower was centrally between nave and choir or at the west end, but they can, in fact, be found in almost any position other than the east end of the church. At Fingest in Buckinghamshire, Brook in Kent and Climping in Sussex (pl. 5), the towers are extremely massive but not particularly tall. Because of the Normans' conservative finance, building often took a long time and one can see the gradual evolution of the Norman style in the same tower, notably at Castor in the Soke of Peterborough. Very occasionally, for example in Melbourne in Derbyshire and St Germans in Cornwall, one finds a pair of towers at the west end, an elegant but expensive arrangement.

In general, the Norman tower was the appropriate accompaniment to a static form of architecture, a vigorous no-nonsense composition with few concessions to charm. But, as was the case with other features, the style later softened and more decoration was added, as can be seen at Castor and at St Peter, Northampton. It is difficult to note any particular regional characteristic, but in various parts of the country there is a kind of circular porthole opening. Although this is more noticeable in the larger churches it can be seen at Old Shoreham in Sussex.

The Normans continued to use the pyramidal cap as a tower covering, particularly in the south-east where it became known as the 'Sussex cap'. Sometimes, however, an unfinished tower has a gabled or saddle-back top. This is found all along the limestone belt in the lias areas (see Chapter 2) and it is significant that this rather modest construction is found in good stone areas but where, agriculturally, the soil is rather poor.

Early English. It seems likely that the spire grew out of the pyramidal cap. The latter construction – low and rather basic – was out of keeping with the new Gothic style of lancet windows, high vaults and pointed arches so that the Early English masons doubtless started to elevate the cap. The beginnings of the process can be studied at Barnack, where the embryonic spire is built of stone with tall polygonal pinnacles at the corners, and at Merstham in Surrey, where the spire is built of wood covered with shingles (small cleft chips of wood, formerly oak but now mostly Canadian cedar). Both date from the beginning of the thirteenth century, but Barnack is the earlier, as well as having what is probably the oldest spire in the country. Gradually, as the builders experimented more, spires became taller. In the timbered areas of the south-east, shingled spires were the normal type; they often overlapped the tower and the corners were chamfered off, giving the impression of a man wearing a hat too big for him. An example of this so-called 'splay-footed' spire from another part of England is Cleobury (pronounced Clebbery) Mortimer in Shropshire (pl. 77).

Apart from shingles, lead could be used to cover a wooden spire. Perhaps the best-known of this type is that at Chesterfield in Derbyshire which is warped and twisted, no doubt owing to the use of unseasoned wood and the melting of the lead by the sun. Examples of lead spires are found in many places, Long Sutton in Lincolnshire, Godalming in Surrey and Hemel Hempstead in Hertfordshire (pl. 13) are just a few. In the last and neighbouring counties there are a number of very narrow lead spirelets recessed within the tower parapets called 'Hertfordshire spikes' or 'snuffers'. Sheathing spires with copper, which made them a conspicuous bright green (Chigwell, Essex, is an example), was not practised before the eighteenth century. Attractive as these timber spires and spirelets are, they cannot compare in dignity with stone spires. The earliest stone group is to be seen in and around Oxford; dating from the thirteenth century, they are characterized by tall massive pinnacles at the corners and large dormer windows at the base.

Towers, in the Early English period, in common with the style generally, show a much greater variety of design and proportion than those of an earlier date. Most were square, although octagonal towers – a sophisticated design probably imported from France – do occur, as does the occasional square tower which changes to an octagon at the top. Projecting stair-turrets are normal but sometimes these are masked by buttresses. Towers are often of lofty proportions, but others are low and massive. There is more decoration, and belfry windows are frequently large. Different types of buttresses also occur, these can embrace the angle (clasping), be placed against the angle and project outwards (diagonal) or meet at right angles at the tower angles (rectangular). A variant of the last, set slightly back and still showing the tower angles, is called 'setback'. The tower was, however, still relatively uncommon, which is hardly surprising as outside the monasteries it was not an age of great wealth, and as we have seen the tower is a luxury.

Decorated. Towers of the Decorated period continued the process of elaboration. There was a growth of architectural detail, such as the provision of parapets, usually with a pinnacle at each corner and sometimes at other points, which adds to the visual pleasure of fourteenth-century steeples. The combination of elegant towers and magnificent spires – perhaps best seen at Louth, Lincolnshire – produces a delightful focal point for many an English town and village.

Round spires are, of course, difficult to construct. The natural shape is octagonal, which involves a transition from the square tower to the octagonal spire. We have seen how this was effected with the shingled or leaded timber spires and in the early stone spires of Oxfordshire where large pinnacles filled the awkward corners.

The next step was to develop the broach. This is a half-pyramid which covers the corner and carries the line of the eye easily from the edge of the square tower to the octagonal spire. Much depends on the relative proportions of the two elements of the steeple and the size of the broach but, as J. Charles Cox writes, 'Early English broach spires were aesthetically as well as structurally one of the supreme achievements of their age.' They often rose to over 150 feet, and some idea of their impact can be gained from the illustration of Spaldwick Church (pl. 45). This is one of the finest of a group in Huntingdonshire, which, together with parts of Lincolnshire, Rutland and Northamptonshire, is the area of the stone spire. Spire-lights, necessary for ventilation, surmounted by little gablets provided a decorative feature but, if too prominent, might give a 'warty' appearance; these were placed on the cardinal faces, or on cardinal and diagonal sides alternately.

Nevertheless, with all its virtues, the broach spire was not as satisfactory as the parapet type which succeeded it in the fourteenth century and which then became the accepted form until spires generally ceased with the development of the Perpendicular style. In this type the spire was erected inside the parapet and did not reach to the edge of the tower or overlap it. Apart from being more pleasing to the eye spires served no functional purpose, although there was the practical advantage that the steeplejack could set his ladders on the top of the tower instead of having to climb from the ground. Sometimes he was further helped by crockets, leaf-shaped projections, which served not only as steps but also as decorative features. Bands were another means of ornamentation.

With the full flowering of the Gothic forms in the Decorated style, spires were at their finest. These tapering constructions were the perfect climax to the architecture of pointed arches and delicate window tracery.

Perpendicular. When the Decorated style gave way to the Perpendicular in the fifteenth century there was a change of emphasis. This period was a time of great prosperity in the wool and cloth trades, and churches in the areas where this trade flourished tended to become more sumptuous. It was realized that the new and glorious towers which were being built did not need spires to complete them. An added reason for dispensing with them was the aesthetic consideration that, owing to the discovery of guttering, roofs had become flatter and their horizontal sweep did not blend with a spire's vertical thrust.

Some thousands of towers were built during the Perpendicular period. Local pride was probably involved and most of the great tower areas, such as Somerset, Gloucestershire, East Anglia and the East Riding of Yorkshire, were regions in which prosperous wool merchants lived. Somerset, in particular, is supreme among English counties in the quality, the number and the variety of its noble towers.

Subsequent development. The Reformation led to a return to Classical forms, seen on the grand scale in Wren's masterpiece – St Paul's Cathedral. Later, in Georgian times, brick came into fashion. Although Wren and his successors evolved the Renaissance steeple, neither development favoured the building of the Gothic type of spire. Apart from the fact that it is almost impossible to build them of brick, the worldly approach of those times left no place for the upward yearning of the spire, and stylistically they were not suited to Classical forms. They came, however, into their own again with the Gothic Revival of Victorian times and there are few towns of any size without a Victorian Gothic spire.

We owe much to the builders of our towers and spires. Indeed, one has only to imagine the skylines of our towns and villages without them to appreciate what they contribute to the visual enjoyment of England. Painters have helped increase this pleasure. Constable, in particular, has left unforgettable impressions with his views of Salisbury and Dedham Vale. Let us hope that the present preference for tall blocks of offices and flats may not lead to their being overshadowed; the English scene would be immeasurably the poorer if they were.

4 COMMUTER COUNTRY

(ESSEX, KENT, MIDDLESEX, SURREY AND SUSSEX)

The south-east, as all who lived through the Battle of Britain will recall, lies in the path of the invader. Julius Caesar, Hengist and Horsa, Aella and William all landed on the shores of Kent and Sussex. Not all, however, came across the sea with a weapon in their hand. A more peaceful and far-reaching penetration took place in 597 when St Augustine landed close to the same spot, Ebbsfleet near Ramsgate, where Hengist and Horsa had come ashore previously. St Augustine's mission (see Chapter 1), was almost immediately successful, although during his lifetime it did not extend beyond the county of Kent. London remained obdurately pagan, and so Canterbury became the focal point of the Christian Church in England instead of the capital, as Pope Gregory wished.

As in the rest of England, most of the pre-Conquest churches that remain date from the last hundred years of Saxon rule. They include two major buildings, a sole survivor of a split-log church, a unique tower and one or two items of lesser interest.

Perhaps the outstanding remaining Saxon church is that of St Nicholas at Worth, on the northern border of Sussex. Nairn has described it as 'one of the most powerful of Anglo-Saxon churches, large in scale and bold in conception'. The massive chancel arch is twenty-two feet high and one of the tallest in the land. High in the nave wall are three baluster shaft openings – a unique position, as normally they only appear in towers.

The other major building is St Mary in Castro, Dover, which, as its name suggests, is located within the walls of the castle. It is an unusually complete cruciform church dating from *c*. 1000 and has a low central tower. As at Worth, the crossing is not a true one, for the nave, chancel and transepts are not of equal height. The chancel and transepts are neither as high nor as wide as the nave, so that the tower rests on the ground and not on the arms.

During one of the many incursions to which England was subject during the six hundred years prior to the Conquest, King Edmund was martyred at Hoxne, Suffolk, in 868 for refusing to renounce his Christianity. One hundred and fifty years later, his body was brought to Greensted, near Ongar, and here is the only remaining example of a church with walls built of oak logs split in half and set vertically on an oak sill. It has been heavily restored, but is an evocative reminder of the timber churches of those days. Here, too, is one of the Essex timber towers which will be discussed later.

The unique tower is the Rhenish helm at Sompting (see Chapter 3), near Worthing. There are nineteenth-century examples – St Peter, Southampton; Wormhill, Derbyshire and Flixton, Suffolk – but Sompting has the only original tower of this type, so common in the Rhineland. The church was later granted to the Templars and then, when they were expelled in 1306, to the Knights Hospitallers.

The lesser delights remaining from this period include Bosham and Bishopstone in Sussex and Lyminge in Kent. The Bayeux Tapestry shows Harold, with hawk on hand, going to hear Mass at Bosham before sailing on his ill-fated visit to Normandy in 1064, and it is probable that the chancel arch, and certainly the lower part of the tower, are as Harold saw them. The chancel arch is one of the best Saxon arches in the country.

Bishopstone, a charmingly secluded church despite its proximity to the built-up areas of Newhaven and Seaford, has a complete Saxon porticus (a side-chamber, rather like an embryonic transept) dating from the eighth century and, in the gable above the south door, a sundial inscribed EADRIC.

Lyminge started life as one of the small churches built by St Augustine and his followers, although today it exhibits late Saxon features. The nave of the contemporary St Cedd's Church remains at Bradwell-juxta-Mare, Essex, lonely and moving by its remote estuary.

Norman. As soon as they could do so, the Norman invaders made their mark in the building of parish churches, not least in the lands they had first overrun. Lanfranc was brought over by William from Normandy to become Archbishop of Canterbury and, in the incredibly short time of seven years, is reported as having rebuilt the cathedral. Kent was one of the most populous counties in the twelfth century and a great deal of Norman work in the south-east still remains, especially in Sussex. This county, in fact, shows all phases of Norman architecture, from the early severity to the later exuberance, culminating in the outstanding Transitional Norman churches of New Shoreham and Steyning.

Since St Dunstan had revived the life of the religious houses in the tenth century, the organization of the Church had been largely monastic. From this developed the institution, peculiar to England, of cathedral priories, where the cathedrals were staffed from the monasteries with a monk as bishop. William encouraged this practice, and, throughout the Middle Ages, about half the cathedrals were governed by a prior and monks, all, except Carlisle, under Benedictine rule.

Monastic life prospered under William and Lanfranc, and the thirty-five Benedictine houses for men and six for women in existence at the time of the Conquest were soon increased. New monastic orders were introduced, first Cluniac, then Augustinian Canons and, later in the twelfth century, the Cistercians.

The buildings were erected in the new Norman style brought from France by the conquerors. This, in turn, exercised considerable influence on the styles used in parish churches, although the impulse behind parish church-building in the Norman period was mainly regal or baronial. Later, in the thirteenth century when the power of the Church was at its height, the impulse became largely monastic.

Monastic influences in the south-east came mainly from Canterbury and the great Cluniac foundation at Lewes, but Battle Abbey and Waltham Abbey were also important. The nave of Waltham, dating from *c.* 1150, is a reminder of the mighty abbey of the Augustinian Canons which existed there until the Dissolution.

There are extensive wall-paintings at Clayton and Hardham and, although the style is not necessarily Cluniac, these churches depended upon Lewes at the time they were painted and it is probable that the inspiration came from the Priory. These paintings are quite exceptional in England for their date and extent, and, in the case of Hardham, for the state of their preservation. There are others at Coombes, West Chiltington (some of later date) and fourteenth-century ones at Trotton, so that Sussex is a good county for murals. These give a fair idea of what a mediaeval church looked like – filled with colour from the wall-paintings and the stained glass which spoke to the largely illiterate congregations of the times in a language they could understand.

Perhaps it is unduly encouraging that at Trotton, where the Seven Deadly Sins and the Seven Acts of Mercy are illustrated in roundels on the west wall, the sins are faded almost beyond recognition while the acts of mercy are still clear. These murals have been most carefully restored but, for those who are prepared to accept repainting, there are two churches in other counties in the area which make little demand on the imagination to decipher the often faded pictures. The apse and most of the nave walls of the small village church of Copford, near Colchester, and the whole of the west wall of the twelfth- to thirteenth-century church at Chaldon, in the Surrey chalk down country, are covered with paintings contemporary with the building of these rural centres of worship. Among other scenes the Chaldon murals depict a rare subject, the Purgatorial Ladder, in which little naked figures, who are unable to ascend far enough up the ladder, are consigned by awesome, fork-wielding demons into a cauldron heated by fierce flames.

Less alarming and quite exquisite is the wall-painting of the Virgin and Child in the middle of the east wall of the chancel at Great Canfield, Essex, described by Pevsner as 'one of the best thirteenth-century representations of the subject in the whole country'.

Coombes and Hardham are typical of the small hamlet churches in which Sussex, particularly west Sussex, abounds. There was little industry in later years and the large estates (Arundel, Cowdray and Petworth) have preserved villages from development, so that the county has an unusually large number of these churches. It is hard to exaggerate the charm of these little buildings with their unaffected simplicity, lack of restoration and delightful furnishings, sometimes situated in a cul-de-sac from which the only exit is to the wide sweep of the South Downs. They are not all Norman but, whatever their age, they have great appeal. There are one or two examples in Surrey, Pyrford (pl. 7) and Wisley (which are both in the same parish), and Farleigh, only four miles from the concrete blocks of Croydon.

Some, such as Didling (pl. 8) and Greatham, are single-celled, that is to say there is no structural division between nave and chancel. Two of these single-celled churches, Little Tey, Essex and North Marden, Sussex, have apses which are believed to be two of only four of this type in England.

Others with apses, but which are not single-celled, are Copford, Hadstock, and, of all unlikely places, East Ham, in Essex.

Kent, too, has Norman village churches, but these are of a different breed and include Barfreston and Patrixbourne, two of the most elaborately decorated small Norman churches in the country. Both have the rare feature of a wheel-window (a circular window with short columns or colonettes as spokes), in each case richly decorated.

Uncommon as wheel-windows are, there is a third in the area, at Castle Hedingham in Essex. This brings us to the larger Norman churches. The impulse behind the building of Castle Hedingham came from the de Veres, one of the most powerful Norman families in England, who lived in the adjacent castle. This large parish church has nave pillars alternately round and octagonal. The original tower is no longer there and the external appearance gives little hint of the impressive interior.

The other major churches in the area are far from complete. Only the naves remain at Waltham Abbey and Steyning; and at the former it is barely a third of the important abbey church that used to exist. Interestingly enough, some of the pillars at Waltham are deeply grooved, like those of Durham Cathedral. Not so very far away from Steyning, at New Shoreham, the choir and one bay of the nave are all that are left.

Steyning and New Shoreham represent the peaks of Norman architecture in the region and can compare with the best Norman parish church work in the country. Both are late and therefore richly ornamented and both were given to monasteries – Steyning by William I to Fécamp, New Shoreham by the local lord to Saumur. The scale is almost metropolitan and how, at New Shoreham, such a large church which was never, in itself, monastic, came to be built is a mystery. Today, truncated like Steyning, it looks perhaps a little faded but still magnificent.

The Norman style was too standardized, too inflexible to lend itself to regional individuality, except for the towers. But it is really in the furnishings, especially the fonts, and the types of decoration that local characteristics appear. There is not much in the towers to catch the eye in the south-east apart from a very uncharacteristic sprinkling of round towers, which seem to have strayed from East Anglia. There are three in Sussex and six in Essex, though some were rebuilt later.

Thirty or so lead fonts still exist in England, and of these, half a dozen Norman and one rare fourteenth-century example are located in this region. The two best are probably at Brookland, in Kent, and Walton-on-the-Hill, Surrey. The former has the Signs of the Zodiac and Labours of the Months in two rows under arcading, the lead being laid in ten vertical strips. Walton-on-the-Hill has a frieze at top and bottom and eight delicately modelled, seated figures in high relief, placed under round-headed arches. They wear haloes and hold books. The lead strip is of one piece and may once have been long enough to include twelve figures, which were probably, despite the number, doctors of the church and not apostles. The other fonts are at Lower Halstow and Wichling in Kent and at Edburton, Parham (the fourteenth-century example) and Pyecombe in Sussex.

In an area with so much Norman work and where one can find churches, large and small, some early, some late, dotted about all over the region, it is difficult to single out more individual items, but it would be inappropriate not to mention New Romney Church, with its ornate western tower, and Corringham's tower in Essex. Nor should one conclude that there is nothing to see in Middlesex, for there is a fine doorway of four orders at Harlington, an arcade at Laleham, much Norman work at East Bedfont and a font at Hendon. The Normans have, in fact, left marks of their vigorous building activity everywhere in the area.

Early English. The Gothic style came to this country with the Cistercians (see Chapter 1), who built their first house at Waverley, near Farnham in Surrey. This is not Cistercian country, however, for, inaccessible as many parts were because of the dense forests, it did not have the remote conditions near water which the order sought. Because of their preference for isolation, it was some time before their ideas on architecture could permeate through to parish churches. Of far greater impact was the rebuilding of the choir of Canterbury Cathedral in the last quarter of the twelfth century by William of Sens. His work was continued by William the Englishman, who, despite his name, was more French than English. These two men brought from France new ideas about architecture and applied them to the cathedral.

It is not surprising, therefore, that there are many fine Early English parish churches in Kent, notably Minster-in-Thanet, Hythe and Westwell. The last is a complete building of this style, and has a rare stone screen and vaulted chancel. Another is Woodchurch, which has an exceptionally tall timber spire covered with shingles. A feature of the county's Early English churches is the decoration of the chancel with arcading and Bethersden marble shafts, either as a dado under the windows or embracing the lancets as well.

Up Marden, in Sussex, is a more modest, but entirely unaltered, village church. Nairn describes it as 'one of the loveliest interiors in England'. Unrestored, little used, but lovingly tended, it lies alone five hundred feet up on the Downs in the west of the county. Near Littlehampton, there is Climping (pl. 5), perhaps the most perfect of thirteenth-century Sussex churches. Sussex, indeed, is a good Early English county as well as a Norman one, and can offer a wide diversity of churches. Boxgrove, a former Benedictine monastery, is quite imposing.

Bosham, already mentioned, has the uncommon feature of a five-light lancet window in the east end. Surrey, however, goes two better at Ockham, which has the almost unique example of a seven-light window, marble-shafted and with finely carved foliage capitals. Perhaps the best thirteenth-century churches as a whole in Surrey are Chipstead and Dunsfold. Chipstead is a large building with crossing tower and transepts, and a fine array of lancets in the chancel and north transept. Dunsfold, in the Wealden part of the county, dates from about 1270 and is an authentic village church of the period, still retaining its mediaeval character. The living at the time was in the possession of the Crown and there is reason to believe that it was built by royal masons. Dunsfold also has some of the oldest benches in the country, installed when the church was erected.

There is not much Early English architecture in Middlesex, but Essex has a good example of a thirteenth-century chancel at Easthorpe.

Decorated. Two of the distinguishing marks of the Decorated style are stone spires and tracery. There are many wooden spires in the south-east, usually sheathed with shingles, although lead was used, for example, at Godalming, Surrey and Harrow, Middlesex. The south-east is not, however, a region for stone spires. Kent, Surrey and Middlesex have none from mediaeval times and Sussex only has five, including the rebuilt one at Chichester Cathedral. Therefore one can hardly call it good Decorated country. On the other hand, Kentish tracery (see p. 267) with split cusps, a well-known variety of the infinite forms of fourteenth-century tracery, is an important characteristic of that county.

The Decorated period and the preceding Early English phase led to the addition of aisles to the basic structure but, in general, the further

44

step of providing clerestories was not adopted in the south-east, even in the succeeding Perpendicular age. Lydd, where Cardinal Wolsey was at one time the rector and which has one of the longest naves and chancels in England, has no clerestory and this product of the later Middle Ages is conspicuous by its absence.

Instead, two methods were adopted to cover the aisles that were then being built. These, for convenience, might be called the 'catslide' and the parallel three-gable solutions. With the catslide, which was more common in Sussex, the roof was brought down in one sweep from the ridge to a few feet above the ground, as at Amberley (pl. 4) and Lyminster. With the three gables, the aisles were extended to the end of the chancel and separately roofed, so that a parallel three-gable effect was created, as at Westerham (pl. 3), Lynsted, Upchurch and New Romney. Although these are all in Kent, the same practice was also used in Cornwall, so that a local feature is common to both the extreme south-east and extreme south-west of England. The reason is not clear; it may be purely a local mannerism, or else there were not the rich wool merchants to provide the funds necessary to build clerestories.

Although there was some opening-up of the Weald in the fourteenth-century, for example Smarden, Kent, the Decorated style is lightly represented in the region and is often lost under later additions. Particularly in Sussex it appears that the masons favoured an austere style and looked askance at the more elaborate treatment of this period. But at Winchelsea, in Sussex, the church was planned on a grand scale to be worthy of a royally conceived new town. Only part of the original remains, but that is enough to arouse admiration.

Perpendicular. The number of Perpendicular churches in any given area depends largely on its prosperity during the fourteenth and fifteenth centuries. Although today the south-east gives an image of affluence, this was not generally the case in mediaeval times. Kent and Middlesex had good soil and the former benefited from its position between London and the Continent, while the latter embraced the capital itself. Surrey and Sussex, on the other hand, were little regarded. The soil was difficult to drain and the thickly wooded Weald afforded abundant cover for vagrants and others who preyed on travellers. So dense were the trees that to travel from Surrey to the Sussex coast it was sometimes necessary to go via Kent. The old Roman highway, Stane Street, which went from

London to Chichester had long since been abandoned and, until the turnpike roads were built in the eighteenth century, communication was worse than in Roman times.

Iron-founding was only on a modest scale, the glass industry was confined to certain areas, such as Albury and Chiddingfold, and the coppices for fencing and hop-poles could not be said to have generated much wealth.

Essex was better placed. It benefited from the wool and cloth trades in the north, to which the churches of Great Bromley, Brightlingsea and Constable's beloved Dedham bear witness, and further south, saffron-growing and the manufacture of cutlery produced the fine churches of Saffron Walden and Thaxted. Parts of Kent also had a breeze of prosperity from the cloth trade, in addition to the income derived from its generally good farming land.

It is only in Middlesex that the tide of affluence seems to have ebbed rather than flowed in the nineteenth century. Its proximity to London, moreover, has resulted in the quiet riverside villages and good alluvial soil being smothered with bricks and mortar and, although fringes of country remain in the north-west and north-east, it has taken on the character of built-up London and its inner suburban areas. London has few mediaeval churches, chiefly due to the Great Fire of 1666 which destroyed all but seven of the hundred churches in the tightly packed square mile of the city. Because London has little to offer in this way it has been left out of our field of study altogether. The rest of Middlesex has minor pleasures.

Surrey and Sussex are not Perpendicular counties. The best church of this style in Surrey is at Lingfield, in the south-east, rebuilt, except for the fourteenth-century tower, by Sir Reginald Cobham when he founded a college of priests there in 1431. Lingfield, however, is on a relatively small scale and does not have a clerestory.

The benefits of the cloth trade in Kent, which was helped by the arrival of Flemings in Edward III's reign, is seen in the church of Cranbrook. The tower is perhaps a little inadequate, but is helped by the later addition of a fine clock. Grander than Cranbrook is the collegiate church of All Saints, Maidstone, completely rebuilt in the Perpendicular period, it has the widest nave of any parish church in England. This, however, is of ragstone and lacks the warm yellow sandstone colouring of Cranbrook.

The towers of Kent, which will be discussed in the next section, are a special feature of the county and contribute greatly to the Kentish scene.

Towers. If the mark of the Decorated period is the stone spire, the Perpendicular phase is distinguished by the wealth of great towers, usually without spires. In common with the lack of great Perpendicular fabrics, Surrey and Sussex are notably deficient in good towers. There is a group in east Sussex, paid for by the Pelham family, and marked with the buckle granted to them after the Battle of Poitiers. In Surrey the best is probably the one at Worplesdon with its prominent stair-turret. Nicely placed on an eminence, it is built of the local heathstone. A number of Middlesex towers also have the turret, from which one might single out Heston. A distinctive feature of four or five churches in the London Airport area is the eighteenth-century addition of a gay little cupola on top, sometimes, as at Harmondsworth (pl. 9), painted in a cheerful blue; it provides a charming eye-catcher in a not very inviting landscape. Cupolas of a different shape occur in east Kent, for example, at Ringwould and Woodnesborough.

Kent has many delightful towers of its own type, also usually with stair-turrets continuing above the top. Seal (pl. 2), near Sevenoaks, is a good example. This type of tower is without pinnacles, but a small group in the south-east, Ashford, Lydd and Tenterden, of which the last is the finest, have this embellishment. There are more than eighty from the Perpendicular period and many of them, such as Newington, make a lovely picture dominating village and orchards or hop-fields.

An unusually large proportion of the towers in the three counties south of the Thames are placed in a flanking position at the side, rather than in what is termed an axial location (Climping tower (pl. 5) is attached to the south transept). This is also found in the south-west, but it is uncommon elsewhere.

Essex is quite different from any other county in its number of late mediaeval brick towers and more rustic but very attractive timber towers. Among the thirty or so brick towers, pride of place must go to Ingatestone (pl. 11), but others of note are Rochford, Layer Marney, Gestingthorpe and Wickham St Paul.

The timber towers rise straight from the ground independently of the nave, and are not supported on framing placed within the main body of the church; they are further braced by raking shores or beams resting at an angle against the upright corner-posts. These, with their covering, form a lean-to aisle or ambulatory around three sides of the tower. The whole looks like a centrally planned church with the tower in the middle and, indeed, is probably the original Saxon wooden church. The timber towers that still exist include Margaretting (pl. 10), Navestock, Blackmore and West Hanningfield. The sturdiness of these homely structures is borne out by the fact that a flying bomb which fell during the Second World War a few yards from Navestock tower failed to topple it.

Stone. New Shoreham Church is built of Caen stone from Normandy. This material is a particular feature of the south-east; it was near to the source of supply and its use was encouraged for political reasons in Norman times. It was more easily obtainable than many English stones and its light tones blended well with the English setting. As noted in Chapter 2, the region as a whole was not well provided with building stone, but one should not overlook the contribution made by the Bargate and Wealden sandstones with their warm, sunny tints, or by the more dour Reigate sandstone and Kentish ragstone. Kent also produced freshwater limestones which will take a polish, of which the best known is Bethersden. There was, of course, chalk-stone and plenty of the flints which go with the chalk; too much, perhaps, for it is easy to tire of this unsympathetic material, especially when it is used in the rough Surrey way without refinements, as compared with the more gracious use of carefully coursed knapped flints in parts of Sussex. A flint exterior, however, can often hide an elegant interior, as Westwell demonstrates, and one must not be put off by its ubiquity in the south-east.

The absence of stone is often partially compensated for by the availability of good clay for brick-making and this is the case in the south-east. Kent is outstanding for the sophisticated use of brick, and houses like Bradbourne, near the Mallings, reach a summit of virtuosity which is hard to equal. For mediaeval architecture, however, and especially church architecture, one must go to Essex. In no other county is there such admirable mediaeval brickwork.

It is curious that, after the departure of the Romans, building in brick lapsed in England for the best part of a thousand years, although there was no similar gap on the Continent. But Essex reverted to this material earlier than any other part of the country. It is highly probable that the brick dressings of Little Coggeshall Abbey were made locally, possibly with the help of Flemish immigrants, as early as 1225 and so would be the earliest mediaeval example in the country. The county, too, had connections with the Netherlands where this form of construction was very highly developed.

Essex was indeed fortunate in these respects, because, other than pudding-stone, a conglomerate of flints and other stones bound together with a natural cement, and a strange substance called septaria, mainly consisting of nodules of clay, the county along with Middlesex is more stoneless than any of the other three. Geologically, it is a very young county, being entirely a product of the Tertiary era (see Chapter 2).

In addition to brick, it had good oak and it was the availability of these two materials that dictated the special character of Essex mediaeval churches. There was, of course, plenty of wood in the counties south of the Thames, as indicated by the countless spires, spirelets and bell-turrets, but the timber towers of Essex (Margaretting, pl. 10) are a local speciality only occasionally found elsewhere in the region, for example Burstow in Surrey and High Halden in Kent. There are fine roofs, too, in the north, and many attractive porches, of which Margaretting again has a good example.

Brasses. Being near to the continental sources of latten, a compound of zinc, lead and tin, which was used for making brasses, Kent shares with Essex and East Anglia the distinction of having more memorial brasses than any other part of England. Cobham has the finest set in the whole country, dating from the best period for brasses. Nineteen different brasses, commemorating members of the de Cobham and Brooke families, also show the development in armour and costume over two centuries. Although there is nothing on this scale in Surrey and Sussex, these two counties possess, respectively, the oldest male and female brasses in the land. The exceptionally fine one at Stoke d'Abernon to Sir John d'Aubernoun dates from 1277, and the other, at Trotton, to Margaret, Lady Camoys dates from 1310.

General. Throughout history this region has been largely dominated by the presence of London, constantly demanding more green space for those who work in it. New towns have grown up as far afield as Crawley in Sussex and Harlow in Essex.

On the other hand, perhaps also due to the proximity of the capital, there is much loving and often affluent care directed towards preserving the rich heritage of parish churches. The Victorians took to the south-east and inflicted lasting harm to unsuspecting places of worship, but today we are, perhaps, more sensitive to the original character of the churches. The region is a great deal more prosperous now than it was in mediaeval times and, even if there are fewer worshippers, the church still remains the focal point of many villages and towns.

The predominant impression is the abundant use of timber, especially for spires, spirelets and bellcotes. The brick of Essex, however, is a precious heritage which occurs nowhere else in such profusion. These materials and the stone towers of Kent provide charming scenes in an area which, despite the number of people who now live in it, is still largely rural, even if seldom remote.

5 SOUTHERN CHALK

(BEDFORDSHIRE, BERKSHIRE, BUCKINGHAMSHIRE, HAMPSHIRE, HERTFORD-
SHIRE, OXFORDSHIRE AND WILTSHIRE)

This region, except on the north-western fringe, is also deficient in good building stone and, other than Oxfordshire, Wiltshire, parts of Berkshire and Hertfordshire, was not particularly wealthy in the Middle Ages. The dominant landscape feature is chalk downland, comfortable and softly rounded, but sometimes with a strange sense of isolation, as in the wide-open spaces of Salisbury Plain and the Marlborough Downs.

Historically, these are some of the oldest parts of England. Wiltshire is probably one of the best-known and richest areas in Europe for Bronze Age and earlier remains. About 3000 BC, Neolithic settlers brought knowledge of agriculture and the raising of stock to Britain. Their chief centre was the famous Windmill Hill site on the hill of that name near Avebury.

Later, in the Bronze Age, immigrants from north Germany established at Stonehenge the celebrated Wessex Culture, and traded the gold and copper of Ireland with continental merchants. The gold for the magnificent Mycenaean treasures may well have passed through the hands of merchants from the area around Stonehenge. This sanctuary is probably the most renowned of its period in the whole of Europe. Built between 1500 and 1400 BC it marks the peak of this culture. The wealth of those who built it is attested by the splendour of the objects that were placed in the burial-mounds with them.

Anglo-Saxon period. Berkshire and Wiltshire were much fought over during the period between the departure of the Romans and the arrival of the Normans. The main population centres of Berkshire – Windsor, Reading, Wallingford, Newbury and Abingdon – commanded fords over the rivers Thames and Kennet. The Mercians struggled for supremacy over Wessex and Alfred contended valiantly, and eventually successfully, with the Danes. Wars make short work of architecture, especially when the buildings are of wood, but despite this, and particularly in Hampshire, there is much to see from pre-Conquest times.

Perhaps the most notable church is All Saints at Wing in Buckinghamshire, which has been described as 'one of the most interesting Anglo-Saxon churches in England'. All Saints is not only large for its date but has aisles; it also has the rare feature of a polygonal apse housing a raised chancel, below which is a *confessio* dating from the second half of the seventh century. A confessio is a crypt with a small central area to receive the relic of a revered saint and encircled by an ambulatory around which pilgrims could process in veneration.

Not far behind in interest is St Mary's at Breamore (pl. 28), in Hampshire – about ten miles south of Salisbury. Wing and Breamore are relatively large churches but St Laurence, at Bradford-on-Avon in Wiltshire, is tiny in comparison. It has an extraordinary story. Until 1856, the church was lost. Hemmed in by buildings, with ordinary house windows inserted in the west front and a chimney-stack rising where the chancel arch used to be, the upper part of the nave was used as a school and the chancel as a cottage. Thanks to his archaeological zest, Canon Jones, the vicar at the time, found in the Bodleian Library a book written by William of Malmesbury, *c.* 1125, which mentioned a little church or *ecclesiola*, built by St Aldhelm at Bradford. It is now believed that St Laurence is Aldhelm's ecclesiola and that this belonged to a monastery. It is an exceptional example of a church built at the beginning of the eighth century which has no post-Conquest alterations. It has both early and late Saxon features, the latter being in the shape of external pilaster strip decoration and reconstructed upper parts. The reconstructed chancel arch measures nine feet eight inches by three feet six inches, and may be one of the smallest in the country. Its height in relation to width is interesting, as is the narrowness of the openings into chancel and side porticus. High up on the eastern nave wall are two famous pieces of sculpture, the flying angels, which may have been connected with a rood. It was the discovery of these which set Canon Jones on his exciting path of discovery.

Also in Wiltshire, in the small village church of Inglesham, near Lechlade, is another intriguing piece of Anglo-Saxon sculpture. This is a Virgin and Child of unusual design, for the legs of the Child are tucked up high.

Pevsner has commented, however, that for pre-Conquest sculpture no county has as much to offer as Hampshire, where there are a number of roods carved in stone. The rood outside the south transept of Romsey Abbey is justly famous. It is most delicately modelled, and shows Christ unattended – except for the hand of God above – in an attitude of victory over death rather than of suffering. This is not all at Romsey; on the south wall of the chancel inside the abbey, there is a small piece of pre-Norman sculpture. This also depicts the Crucifixion but, in this case, Christ is attended by the Virgin Mary and St John, with the Roman soldiers standing below. Also notable are the roods at Breamore and at Headbourne Worthy, near Winchester, which is more than life-size. Both, unfortunately, have the figures hacked off, presumably a relic from the Church's more troubled past. Langford, in Oxfordshire, is another church with two roods, both on the south porch.

Another item of sculpture deserving mention is a gravestone in the form of a Roman altar at Whitchurch, near Andover, showing a half-figure of Christ.

Returning to the actual structure of churches, Bedfordshire has two Saxon towers, at St Peter, Bedford, and Clapham. The former, once a west, is now a crossing tower. Clapham, still a west tower, is unbuttressed and typifies the 'rugged vigour' mentioned in Chapter 3. The churches of the city of Oxford demonstrate every style, and include St Michael's, a church with a Saxon tower. In Hampshire many beguiling village churches remain, among them Boarhunt near Portsmouth, and Corhampton, and Little Somborne near Stockbridge. The last is a single-celled hamlet-type building akin to those of Sussex.

Norman. Again in this region, Hampshire has the best examples of Norman church building. Winchester Cathedral, Romsey Abbey and Christchurch Priory make a trio of memorable Norman buildings which would be hard to match, but one is a cathedral and the other two did not start life as parish churches. There are many other notable Norman churches in the region. Malmesbury Abbey in the north-west of Wiltshire and Dunstable Priory in Bedfordshire are late Norman buildings of the stature of Steyning and New Shoreham in Sussex. Like them, they are also truncated portions of their former selves, having lost their choirs. Malmesbury has exceptionally fine late Norman carving showing an angel flying horizontally over the seated figures of the apostles who, apart from ducking their heads, appear to be taking it all very calmly. The church of St John at Devizes, Wiltshire, has a Norman crossing tower, oblong in shape, and many other twelfth-century structural features. However, as one enters, it is the chancel, low and vaulted with a riot of decoration, that catches the eye. One might expect to have to travel far to see another and yet only a quarter of a mile away is a second example, St Mary's, although not quite so exuberant as St John's.

The show-piece of Oxfordshire is Iffley, now almost part of Oxford. This is late Norman at its most lavish, especially on the west front. Iffley and Stewkley, in Buckinghamshire, are two more of the churches with circular windows.

Portchester, near Portsmouth, is a genuine example of a largely unaltered building of the 1130s. The long unaisled nave is almost claustrophobic, but the west front is impressive with an elaborate doorway of three orders and varied decoration. At Petersfield (pl. 27), the Norman work at the east end of the nave, which at one time formed part of a crossing tower, is particularly striking. Even more spectacular is the church at East Meon, described by Pevsner as 'one of the most thrilling village churches in Hampshire'. It nestles up against the South Downs and is crowned with a short leaded spire. Inside, the church possesses one of the few Tournai marble fonts still in existence in England.

Upton, in Buckinghamshire, is another village church similar to Stewkley. Upton, in the somewhat unlikely town of Slough, consists of nave and chancel with central tower. Both Stewkley and Upton have vaulted chancels, unusual for village churches of the period. Fingest has a huge Norman tower with double saddleback roof, so large in relation to the small church attached to it that it is thought it may at one time have contained the whole church or at least the nave – compare Brook in Kent.

Hertfordshire has a number of churches with apses, such as Bengeo. Manningford Bruce in Wiltshire also has this feature, as well as a charming nineteenth-century addition of a bell-turret with lead spirelet. Hertfordshire has several fine towers; and for spires, the town church at Hemel Hempstead (pl. 13) with its lead-sheathed spire soaring nearly two hundred feet is particularly fine.

Other towers in the region also include the anomaly of a round tower at Great Shefford in Berkshire, far indeed from the East Anglian home of round towers. Other items of interest in Berkshire are the complete and lovable village church at Avington and the vigorous tympanum at Charney Bassett, which shows a man grappling with two gryphons.

Fonts. As noted in the previous chapter, Norman architecture, except for the towers and fonts, did not give much scope for regional individuality. There is much to note, however, in the fonts of this area.

Hampshire has no less than four of the eight surviving Tournai marble fonts referred to in Chapter 1. One is in Winchester Cathedral; the other three are at East Meon, St Michael's, Southampton and St Mary Bourne in the north. The non-Hampshire examples are in Suffolk and Lincolnshire. Winchester Cathedral's font depicts scenes from the legends of St Nicholas – the resuscitation of a drowned youth, and the saving of the three daughters of an impoverished nobleman from a life of prostitution by presenting them with three golden globes. East Meon's font, executed *c.* 1130–40, is finely carved with scenes from the story of Adam and Eve.

Interesting as these furnishings are, they must be rated as shop-work of not perhaps very high artistic merit. More attractive are the Aylesbury fonts. The prototype, at Aylesbury itself, is described in Chapter 1, and about a dozen of this type of font are scattered around this part of Buckinghamshire.

These two types can be considered as a regional speciality, but there are others more widespread which are worthy of note. Stanton Fitzwarren in Wiltshire has an example of the virtues and vices type, in which the eight vices, trampled on and using Latin names, are contrasted with the eight corresponding virtues, for example, Modestia with Inebrietas. Avington has a good Norman tub-type font; and both Childrey and Dorchester have lead fonts.

Monastic Influence. Even mightier than the Norman houses at Romsey (which belonged to the Benedictines) and Christchurch (of the Augustinian order) were St Albans in Hertfordshire and Reading in Berkshire. The Benedictine abbey of St Albans was one of the most important monastic establishments of mediaeval England – rich, powerful and with wide-ranging powers. Sadly, however, it was mismanaged and the tenants antagonized by its unreasonable exactions. It was, therefore, unable to give a coherent architectural lead to buildings which might normally have been influenced by its dominance. Nevertheless much of its early Norman work, huge and forbidding in its severity, remains to show its importance and today forms part of the cathedral which has the most elevated site of any episcopal centre in England. The Cluniac abbey of Reading was founded by Henry I in 1121, and fourteen years later this monarch, who much favoured the abbey, was buried before the high altar. Consecration was performed in 1164 by Thomas à Becket in the presence of Henry II whose rash outburst led to Becket's murder six years later. This powerful abbey was also the scene of Queen Matilda's burial and of John of Gaunt's marriage but, although its influence must have been very great, practically nothing of the fabric remains today.

Abingdon Abbey was constantly involved in disputes with local townspeople and traders because it had the special privilege of holding a street market. In 1327 it was plundered by the outraged citizens and some of the monks killed, but despite these troubles it seems to have revived and become wealthy again.

These monastic foundations and Dunstable, the most important abbey in Bedfordshire, all go back to Norman or earlier times. In Hampshire are the remains of two Cistercian abbeys, isolated in the manner typical of this order. These are the evocative and not sufficiently-known ruins of Netley Abbey and the better-known but not so considerable ruins of Beaulieu.

Early English. The monastic refectory at Beaulieu is still largely intact, with its beautiful staircase leading up to the reading pulpit of which only the bracket survives. This former dining-hall, now the parish church, is a lovely example of pure Early English.

These monastic remains, to which must be added the exceptionally fine north porch of Christchurch Priory, are the main Hampshire contributions to the Early English style, but East Wellow (pl. 29), near Romsey, is a good example of a village church of the time.

Possibly the finest church of this period in the whole area is Felmersham (pl. 15) in Bedfordshire. It is a mystery how a building of this scale came to be in such a small place, but Felmersham did come under

Lenton Priory, the most important monastic foundation in Nottingham-shire when it was built. However this may be, the church is an astonishing *tour de force* and the west front is spectacular.

Uffington, Berkshire, with its octagonal tower, always a mark of sophisticated construction, and a fine south porch, is almost as good. Perhaps, however, the outstanding Early English county in this down-land region is Wiltshire, hardly surprising in a county which boasts Salisbury Cathedral. Potterne and Bishops Cannings were built on manors belonging to the bishops of Salisbury and both were collegiate. They are cruciform with crossing towers and Potterne is a singularly pure example of this style. Boyton has a striking south chapel with its west window of bar tracery, the earliest appearance of this feature in these parts.

It is noticeable that, whereas thirteenth-century naves often have later additions to accommodate increased congregations and provide more altar space, chancels often retained their original proportions. They were, of course, for the officiating priests and there was no prac-tical reason to enlarge them, quite apart from the fact that the rector whose responsibility they were, may not have had the means or the desire to do so. There are a number of these unaltered chancels in Buckinghamshire. In addition, Aylesbury and Haddenham have thirteenth-century towers.

The main attractions in Buckinghamshire are, however, the stiff-leaf capitals which one finds on the Buckinghamshire/Bedfordshire border. Stiff-leaf is an early form of foliage decoration, stylistic and not yet natural but, nevertheless, a charming accompaniment to the pure architecture of this first phase of Gothic. Perhaps nowhere else can this deeply undercut foliage decoration be seen to better advantage than at Eaton Bray (which also has a fine Early English font). Its appearance in this fairly remote village near the Whipsnade Zoo was due to the influence of the local lord, but, even so, would not have been possible with-out the presence of a skilled group of stonemasons in the vicinity. This, no doubt, is the reason why there is so much of this form of ornamentation in such a small area. It can be seen at Ivinghoe, Marsh Gibbon, Pitstone and Wingrave on the Buckinghamshire side of the county boundary and at Studham, Chalgrave and Elstow on the Bedfordshire side.

There is also much excellent ironwork, for example on the south door of Eaton Bray, which probably comes from the workshop where

Thomas of Leighton, the famous maker of the railings round Queen Eleanor's monument in Westminster Abbey, was trained. Another justly famed piece of iron work is to be seen on the north door of Little Hormead church in neighbouring Hertfordshire.

Hertfordshire is in rather a minor key for Early English. The chancel and transepts of Anstey, especially the south one which looks well from the outside with its dignified lancets, are good examples of the style, as is Baldock with its fine west tower. Hatfield's chancel and transepts, the chancel arches of Eastwick and Standon, the early nave arcade of Kimpton and Gilston's late thirteenth-century screen are other pleasures.

Spires. Although the great spire area is the east Midlands, there are some fine mediaeval spires in this region. Oxfordshire, in particular, possesses several early thirteenth-century spires of a distinctive type. The awkward space between the angles of the square tower and the sides of the octagonal spire is filled with pinnacles, the base of which is taken up with a large dormer window but without spire-lights further up. Among the 'dreaming spires' of the city of Oxford, the cathedral spire is of this type and may be the oldest true spire in the country. Other examples are to be seen at Bampton, Broadwell and Witney. The Decorated period is well represented at Adderbury, one of Oxfordshire's finest churches, Bloxham and St Mary the Virgin, Oxford.

There are a number of spires in north Bedfordshire, as at Sharnbrook, and a score in Wiltshire. The other counties can muster only a few. This is surprising in the case of Buckinghamshire, for it adjoins Northampton-shire, the finest spire county in England. There is Olney and Hanslope, rebuilt in Victorian times, and Berkshire has Shottesbrooke.

Decorated. Oxfordshire is a good Decorated county but it is not to be expected that the other parts of the region, where mediaeval spires are in relatively short supply, will be strong in works of this period, although they do occur here and there throughout the area. However, for those who are prepared to seek out the unending variety of Decorated window tracery, there is much to discover – for instance, the east windows of Emberton and Edlesborough in Buckinghamshire, the flowing tracery of Shottesbrooke in Berkshire, and the well-known Jesse window of Dorchester church in Oxfordshire, one of the most famous examples of fourteenth-century tracery in the country.

The abbey church at Dorchester is basically of the Decorated period, although much Victorianized. It also has features from other periods, including a lead font and corbel showing monks asleep during the lengthy mediaeval offices. Hanslope in Buckinghamshire is a good example of the widening of aisles which went on extensively in the fourteenth century and Olney has a fine spacious interior. Emberton also has good Decorated work. In north Oxfordshire, several churches have capitals composed of human busts with interlinked arms, for example, Hampton Poyle (pl. 21).

Further south, in the centre of Buckinghamshire, Edlesborough (pl. 19) makes a fine sight on its isolated hill, while nearby is Ivinghoe (pl. 18), a noble church. In Bedfordshire, Dean, Langford and Swineshead have architecture of this period. Dean, which is quite a small church, has a good timber roof complete with flying angels, but this belongs to the fifteenth century. Marston Moretaine has a detached tower, which is unusual for these parts.

There is much elaborate vaulting in a number of Wiltshire churches (for example, Bishopstone, near Urchfont). Notable chancels were built at Downton, Tisbury and, above all, Edington, where the lovely Decorated work heralds still more exciting things in the next style.

Dorchester has its Jesse window, and, at the east end of Christchurch Priory, the tree of Jesse is depicted in stone on what is, arguably, the finest carved reredos in England. Jesse sleeps at the bottom, hand supporting head, while Solomon and David, with fingers on his harp strings, sit on each side. The Vine spreads upwards, bearing its leaf and full fruit to Mary, to whose Son the Wise Men are offering their presents. As J. R. Wise comments, 'if the reader can imagine the stone reredos as it once was, shining with gold and colour, all its niches filled with statues, and the windows above blazing with crimson and purple . . . he will have some faint idea of the former glory of this Church.' Bampton, in Oxfordshire, also has a stone reredos.

Other furnishings of note include the font canopy at Luton, Bedfordshire, one of only four in England with completely enveloping legs; two monuments at Clifton Reynes, Buckinghamshire, in oak, an unusual material to use; and various wall-paintings, for example, Chalgrove, Oxfordshire and Idsworth, Hampshire.

The change to the Decorated style did not necessarily mean greater display in village churches. Plates 16 and 17 show two country churches which combine fourteenth- with thirteenth-century work. Although from a similar period, they show the infinite variety of our churches. Compton Beauchamp (pl. 17), in Berkshire, is built of a very white chalkstone, giving it a fresh, well-laundered appearance; Shelton, in Bedfordshire, constructed of local grey Totternhoe chalkstone and rubble, makes a dull contrast. Inside, however, they both have the same, unaffected simplicity, greatly helped at Shelton by the clear glass and sensitive restoration.

Perpendicular. The thin soil of chalk does not make for rich agricultural land and although the exceptional purity of the streams which drain through it may produce good pasture and clear water for growing crops like water-cress, this was not enough in the Middle Ages to create wealth. In Hampshire, the chalk dips below later formations before reappearing again in the Isle of Wight. It has given rise to the agriculturally poor but scenically rich woods and moorlands of the New Forest, as well as a rather dull coastline.

Wiltshire and north Oxfordshire were, however, prosperous in the fifteenth and sixteenth centuries; so, too, were parts of Berkshire, where the generally poor economy was relieved by the cloth trade. Jack of Newbury, a self-made cloth merchant and entertainer of Henry VIII, is a typical figure. Hertfordshire, another county which benefited from the cloth trade, also drew economic strength from intensive cultivation, including the growing of barley, which led to malting becoming a particular speciality. Here, as elsewhere, the best Perpendicular churches are in the zones of economic wealth.

The best stone, oolitic limestone, was found in north-west Wiltshire and north Oxfordshire, which are in the limestone belt (see Chapter 2). The building of Salisbury Cathedral was helped by the presence of a pocket of oolite, some way from the main belt, at nearby Chilmark. At Tisbury there is another but, apart from Wiltshire, the chief building materials of the area are chalk and the flints that go with this youngest of the limestones. Only towards the fringes, in Wiltshire and the Isle of Wight, are there older sandstone and limestone formations. Isle of Wight limestone, together with limestone from Dorset, was floated across the sea into Christchurch Harbour and up the River Avon for the building of the priory there.

One must add the curious heath stone or sarsens, sometimes called 'grey wethers' because of their resemblance to recumbent sheep. These are the hard remains of grey sandstone deposits, the rest of which has weathered away. They are much used in the Vale of the White Horse and form a large proportion of the stones used at Stonehenge. In the east of Berkshire, a dark brown conglomerate is to be seen at Binfield and in the tower of Wokingham church.

As the foregoing suggests, the north-west of Wiltshire and the north of Oxfordshire enjoyed the twin advantages of good stone and prosperity in the fifteenth and sixteenth centuries, and here, as one would expect, there are some notable late Gothic buildings, of which the *pièce de résistance* is Steeple Ashton, in Wiltshire. Here, and at neighbouring Trowbridge and Westbury, we can see what the cloth trade could do to provide stately architecture. These churches were completely rebuilt in the sixteenth century. Westbury, and especially Trowbridge, suffer from wholesale later restoration. Steeple Ashton, however, is the genuine article – pinnacles are everywhere, it is battlemented and, apart from nave and tower, stone-vaulted throughout. It is, indeed, a very sumptuous building. The north aisle was paid for by Robert Long and the south by Walter Leucas, both clothiers. The church tower is still forceful enough to show how the village got its name. But, until 1670, when it was blown down, it was finished off with a spire rising to 186 feet.

There are many other signs of Wiltshire's prosperity during the Perpendicular period. The names and donations of wealthy clothiers are linked with St Thomas, Salisbury, Westwood and Great Chalfield (pl. 26). In the last case, Thomas Tropenell, the clothier concerned, built himself a fine stone mansion, and the little church, with its box-like stone bellcote and crocketed spirelet, makes a delightful group with the manor. Calne, the bacon centre, has another notable town church and Lacock, a village one.

The above is an impressive list, but it omits Edington, one of the most important of Wiltshire's churches, and one to which Pevsner applies the adjective 'wonderful'. This church, in the west of the county, has already been mentioned in the Decorated section. It is, like Swanton Morley in Norfolk, one of the outstanding early Perpendicular churches in the country and provides a most interesting link with the earlier style. The reasons for its splendour are not far to seek. The Bishop of Winchester, who came from Edington, and the Black Prince, who wanted a foundation for an order of canons, were the moving spirits behind the building of this church, with its complicated dedication to St Mary, St Katherine and All Saints. This place of worship is a superb and possibly unique example of a building erected in the middle of the fourteenth century, only a few years after the horrors of the Black Death.

Another local feature is the stone chancel screen, a stylish furnishing found in ten Wiltshire churches, for example Compton Bassett, although not confined to this county. Devon, better known for its wooden screens, has fifteen.

Although Oxfordshire is stronger in Decorated work than in Perpendicular, this county has, nevertheless, some good examples. The fan-vault of North Leigh; the well-harmonised group of school, almshouses and church at Ewelme with its magnificent monument and fine roofs; the noble chancel of Adderbury and the smaller churches of Combe and Minster Lovell (pl. 20) are all delightful examples of work of this period. In general this county does not have churches completely rebuilt in the new style but, rather, gradual additions have been made to the original structure. Burford is the classic case of a slow-growth church showing all styles. Idbury is an example of a church with an added clerestory but no aisles.

Jack's church at Newbury, in Berkshire, is an instance of a church entirely rebuilt in the Perpendicular period. It was the scene of the trial of the Newbury Martyrs in Mary's reign and acted as guardroom, hospital and prison during the two battles of Newbury in the Civil War. Abingdon is also of this style, while Shrivenham has a fifteenth-century crossing tower and Radley, strangely for that time and place, a nave arcade of timber.

In Buckinghamshire, Hillesden provides an example of a completely embattled church almost entirely rebuilt in the fifteenth century. The chancel and chapel are richly panelled and the north porch has superlative fan-vaulting. Not far away is something more unusual. Maids' Moreton, as the name suggests, almost certainly owes its construction to two spinsters, the daughters of Sir Thomas Peover, who held a considerable estate in the village. The whole church was built in 1450 and, apart from the addition of a vestry, has remained unaltered. It is a singularly pure example of Perpendicular architecture, and has a much cherished look about it.

This relatively meagre contribution, however, would lead one to suppose – correctly, in my view – that Berkshire and Buckinghamshire are not strong in fifteenth- and sixteenth-century work. But, with one of those anomalies so frequent in England, one could claim that, in the chapel of Eton College and the chapel of St George's, Windsor, a mile away on the other side of the Thames, we reach the peak of this style, although, admittedly, neither is a parish church.

Hertfordshire, which adjoins the wool and cloth areas, can show typical Perpendicular buildings at Ashwell and Baldock. Ashwell is an early example, having been built in the fourteenth century. Other churches are Ware, Watford and Hitchin, the last being noted for its wood screens and roofs.

In Bedfordshire, complete churches of this period are to be found at Toddington, Totternhoe (home of the local grey chalkstone), Flitton and Willington. The last was built by Sir John Gostwick, who had the intriguing title of Treasurer of the First Fruits and Tenths in Henry VIII's reign. Flitton, with its rust-brown colour, and Willington with its buff stone illustrate some of the delightful colour variations that one finds in England.

Hampshire is not a Perpendicular county. One cannot, however, omit the exceptionally fine sixteenth century chancel of Christchurch Priory with its amusing set of misericords, including one which dates from 1220–25 and so is one of the oldest in the country. The Lady Chapel behind probably dates from about 1400. Carisbrooke, on the Isle of Wight, and Barton Stacey have relatively good west towers and Basing is an interesting example of a church built mostly of brick in this style.

Towers. Professor F. J. Allen, in his classic work on the great church towers of England, describes the tower of Christchurch as 'the only considerable tower' in Hampshire, but devotes a whole chapter to Wiltshire towers. Although this does not mean that the whole county is blessed with great towers, the parts that border on Somerset and Gloucestershire partake of their greatness. Many are crossing towers.

Professor Allen singles out a group, which he calls the Westwood group, of which Westwood, with hexagonal stair-turret and ogee cupola, is the outstanding example. They are all built of oolitic limestone and therefore enjoy the advantage of this noble material. The others are St James at Devizes, Nettleton, Yatton Keynell and West Kington. Colerne is of a different design, but nevertheless handsome.

There is also a group – St Sampson at Cricklade, Ss Peter and Paul at Marlborough, and Mere – with octagonal buttresses.

Elsewhere, the best towers are again in the areas touched by cloth prosperity – Ashwell, the outstanding Hertfordshire tower 176 feet high, and Baldock, of the early fourteenth century. Both are crowned with octagonal lanterns and topped by a Hertfordshire spike. Ashwell suffers from being built from a perishable stone and in having a rather blunt top stage. The pinnacled tower of St Nicholas, Newbury, is a restrained design with a large window at the base, single small window in middle and twin larger ones in the top stage. Aldenham, Hertfordshire (pl. 14), is an example of a shingled spire. Buckinghamshire's major tower is Hanslope which, with its spire, was at one time two hundred feet high. It has tall, polygonal pinnacles connected by flying buttresses to the spire. Its striking appearance and that of the tower and fourteenth-century spire of nearby Olney are doubtless due to the proximity of Northamptonshire, the 'county of spires and squires'. The unusual small tower at Maids' Moreton might also be mentioned.

The survey of Perpendicular church architecture in the area can be completed with two Reading towers – St Laurence and St Mary – and that at Henley on Thames, Oxfordshire. The three have a family resemblance in the use of octagonal buttresses, but Henley has no spirelets on top of these. St Laurence is a dignified design with single windows of varying size in each of the three stages.

Monuments. Although largely outside the mediaeval period, a word must be said about Oxfordshire monuments because probably no other county in England has such a wealth and variety of fine sculpture in its memorials. As K. A. Esdaile points out in the *Shell Guide to Oxfordshire*, the county 'is a stone county, rich in the work of native masons for whom the University provided patrons and a training ground well into the eighteenth century; rich in wealthy families who were prepared to go outside the county if they could not find what they wanted locally and which in turn influenced the style of the local masons.'

The monument at Ewelme to Chaucer's grand-daughter, Alice, Duchess of Suffolk, has been rated one of the finest pre-Reformation monuments in the whole country. It has fan-vaulting and is exquisitely carved.

There are several post-Reformation monuments in Oxfordshire, notably the Knollys monument at Rotherfield Grays (pl. 22), the Spencer monument at Yarnton and the Fettiplace monument at Swinbrook. The group of the Fettiplace family at Swinbrook are arranged in tiers of three looking like 'proud sturgeon'. At Stanton Harcourt is an especially fine seventeenth-century Baroque monument to two members of the Harcourt family (pl. 25).

General. We have been dealing with a region of much natural beauty. The Chiltern Hills, often clad with noble beeches, extend through north Hertfordshire, south Bedfordshire, central Buckinghamshire, south Oxfordshire and Berkshire, dropping down to the Buckinghamshire/Berkshire border to produce some of the most spectacular river scenery in the land, while the New Forest and the Isle of Wight contain scenery which draws immense crowds every summer. London still makes its presence felt in Buckinghamshire, Berkshire and Hertfordshire, but, elsewhere, its influence is less apparent, and on parts of the Downs a sense of solitude can still be felt.

6 ENGLISH LOWLANDS

(CAMBRIDGESHIRE, LINCOLNSHIRE, NORFOLK AND SUFFOLK)

The areas already discussed have had examples of fine church building, but here, in the English lowlands which nowhere rise to more than five hundred feet, is the peak of parish church architecture. It is an area of wide skies and distant horizons, where wind and water have made a big impact on the lives of the inhabitants.

In the fenlands of north Cambridgeshire and the fens and marshlands of west Norfolk and south-east Lincolnshire, people settled on islets which were above the large expanses of ground subject to inundation. The conditions must have been similar to the *terpenlands* in Friesland across the North Sea where, years ago, the inhabitants clung to the *terps* or mounds as the only places where it was possible to live.

There is an affinity between these English and Dutch areas and it was Dutch engineers, like Vermuyden, who were invited in the seventeenth century to come over and apply their experience to reclaiming land from the waters. With the aid of the windmill and the construction of dykes, they succeeded and, in so doing, created some of our most fertile land.

Only Wicken Fen remains to remind us of what it was like before the land was drained, but there is still a curious enchantment about these lowlying areas which it is hard to resist. It is not surprising that the Dutch landscape painters, such as the Ruysdaels and Hobbema, had such a great influence on Crome, Constable and Gainsborough.

Suffolk is an agricultural county. Norfolk, too, is mainly concerned with growing things rather than making them. It was sheep, however, that caused such a legacy of fine buildings. The great age of prosperity was stimulated by the arrival of Flemish weavers in the reign of Edward III (1327–77) and the zenith was reached in the fifteenth and early sixteenth centuries.

Building materials will be discussed later, but the noble East Anglian churches arose in an area where only flint, the least urbane of materials, was available and only in Lincolnshire was wealth allied with geology to combine in a summit of architectural virtuosity which is perhaps unequalled in any other county.

Anglo-Saxon. Much, if not all, of this region was Danelaw, as borne out by the frequency of place-names ending with *by* or *thorpe*, and it may well be that the round towers and the astonishing roofs of East Anglia stem from this influence. Anyone who has been to Norway will know of the extraordinary skills in wood shown in the stave churches there.

Despite the number of round towers (112 in Norfolk, 41 in Suffolk and 2 in Cambridgeshire), which are more frequent in the east than the west of the region, there is remarkably little from the Anglo-Saxon period. The Danish invasions wreaked much havoc. North Elmham, in Norfolk, is one of the best examples of a Saxon cathedral that remains, despite the scanty ruins. One can study the masonry, and follow the T-shaped plan with towers placed in the angles of the transepts and nave. The Normans removed the sees to the towns and, indeed, the remoteness of this site for a cathedral is remarkable.

Lincolnshire has most to offer. The church at Stow has the largest and most powerful chancel arch in the country (pl. 44). The whole of the crossing and the transepts are Saxon and, with the exception of Norton in County Durham, the crossing is the only one in England from pre-Conquest times where the arches of the transepts are as high and wide as those of the nave and chancel. The crossing arches are thirty feet high and, therefore, make even Worth in Sussex seem small by comparison. It is surprising to find that the Saxons built on such a scale, especially when one contrasts this with the comparatively small cathedral of North Elmham.

The next most important survival is the tower of St Peter's, Barton-upon-Humber, which was at one time the central portion of a Saxon church, consisting of nave, tower and chancel. It has pilaster strip decoration similar to that at Earls Barton in Northamptonshire, and the top stage has tall twin bell-openings with shafts, a frequent Lincolnshire motif. The other Lincolnshire survivals are all towers – tall, unbuttressed west towers mainly in Lindsey but also in Kesteven and Holland. It seems likely that they were refuges. Broughton tower has a rounded staircase to the west, also found in Northamptonshire at Brigstock and Brixworth.

Saxon church architecture in the rest of Norfolk (other than North Elmham), the whole of Cambridgeshire and Suffolk can be summed up by referring to four towers – the lower part of the west one at Debenham, Suffolk, the one at St Benet's, Cambridge and the central towers of Newton and Weybourne in Norfolk.

Norman. The Isle of Ely was the last part of the country to stand up to William, and the story of Hereward the Wake has entered into English folk-tales. It was not until 1070 that this part was finally subdued and at Ely, where the last resistance was made, the Normans concentrated their building upon the great Benedictine monastery which later became a cathedral. This and Norwich, another monastic foundation, are the main Norman works in the area. But, among parish churches, Ickleton in Cambridgeshire, Castle Rising (the west façade), Tilney All Saints and Walsoken in Norfolk, and Freiston, Deeping St James, Bourne, Long Sutton and Old Leake in Lincolnshire are outstanding.

The most important Norman parish church in Lincolnshire, however, is Stow. Apart from the Saxon chancel arch and transepts, Early English windows in the transepts and the Perpendicular tower, this is a major large Norman building, restored sensitively by J. L. Pearson, a Victorian architect.

From the others, one must single out Walsoken and Ickleton. The seven-bay nave arcade of Walsoken has alternate octagonal and round pillars (like Waltham) and, like Steyning, New Shoreham and Malmesbury, is late. The rest of the church is Gothic. Ickleton, on the other hand, is early – so early, in fact, that the nave arcades rest on Roman monolithic columns. The clerestory is of the same date and, although the church might be reckoned as one of the best early Norman buildings in the country, it is little known. Other Cambridgeshire Norman works are the round towers of Snailwell and Bartlow, and the doorways of Duxford and Pampisford.

Suffolk is not a good Norman county, though the reasons for this are not clear. The Benedictine abbey of Bury St Edmunds was one of the most powerful in the country, ranking with Glastonbury, St Albans, Ely and Norwich. One might have expected that, for such an important place, more Norman influence would remain. It may be that the prosperity of the fifteenth and sixteenth centuries, and the surge of building activity that went with it, swept away much of the Norman work. There are the round towers, of which Little Saxham is the finest, Wortham the largest and Bramfield the only detached one, but these are mainly in the north-east. Otherwise there are a few doorways and the curiosity of the brick arches in nave and clerestory at Polstead. These may have been locally made, and are as early or possibly even earlier than Little Coggeshall.

Early English. Suffolk is weak in Early English church-building, though the riches of the Perpendicular were to redress this. The north chapel and chancel of Mildenhall are the highlights and it is possible that the former, built of limestone and not of flint, may have been the work of a mason from Ely. The chancel is graced by a noble arch at one end and a magnificent window dating from about 1300, which also has an unusual border of quatrefoil circles.

After this there is an anticlimax, but the tower of Rumburgh, once a priory, is noteworthy. There is, too, a minor local feature, of placing piscinas in the angle of a chancel south window. This is quite common and also occurs in Norfolk.

By contrast, Norfolk has a building which is of national importance at West Walton, in the marshlands just across the border from Cambridgeshire, only four miles from Walsoken. The lack of secure foundation made it necessary to build the admirable tower, which acts as a lychgate, sixty feet away from the main fabric, which lies back from the road. Here again are stiff-leaf capitals, of a comparable quality to those at Eaton Bray. The nave arcades with Purbeck marble shafts, sometimes renewed in wood because of lack of money, the stone-flagged floor, and the tall clerestory make as clear an impression of what a church looked like in the middle of the thirteenth century as one can hope to find. Fortunately the restorers have been kept far away.

Great Yarmouth is the largest of all Early English parish churches, but was badly damaged in the Second World War and is now only a pale reflection of what it once was. The west front remains to speak of its former glory, but perhaps in not such a telling manner as the façade of Binham Priory, which may be the earliest thirteenth-century west front in England, even earlier than Westminster Abbey. The huge west window, with its two large lights and quatrefoil circle above, is filled in and the sides are in ruins, but the impact of the acutely pointed arches is clearly felt and is a reminder of the clarity of this style.

Chancels at Burgh-next-Aylsham, Great Cressingham, Wrampling-ham and Blakeney (rib-vaulted), the south porch of Great Massingham and the double piscinas of Hardingham and Pulham St Mary are the also-rans in Norfolk, but still worthy of a detour. However, there is little decorative treatment in Early English churches in Norfolk.

The main features in Lincolnshire are towers and spires. But the district of Lindsey has, at Bottesford, a church demanding special attention. Allowing for a chancel rebuilt in the seventeenth century, a Victorian front to the south transept and a Perpendicular top to the much pin-nacled tower (there was once a spire), it is a remarkably complete example of an Early English cruciform church with west tower. Dog-tooth (decoration in the form of raised stars) is used a great deal, the nave arcade has seats round the bases of the pillars (one of the earliest amenities for the congregation) and on the south side are rings round the shafts, a common thirteenth-century form of decoration. A curiosity, although of much later date, is that the sanctus bell is made of bronze.

In Lincoln Cathedral, with its Angel Choir, the Early English style can fairly be said to have reached perfection. As one would expect, this is reflected in the county's parish churches, particularly at Grantham, a contender for a place in the top dozen of any period. But Grantham's greatest interest is the gradual ripening of Early English into Decorated and, above all, in the elaboration of tracery forms. Great Grimsby and Deeping St James are unusual in that a wall passage is placed im-mediately above the nave arcades and in front of the clerestory, instead of below it and in a separate gallery.

In Cambridgeshire, one would go to Histon and Cherry Hinton to see the best examples of Early English – Histon for its transepts and Cherry Hinton for its chancel, ashlar-faced and a product of the style at its finest. Although much of the window tracery in the transepts of Histon is Perpendicular, the arches are deeply moulded in the Early English style and the shafts have annular rings; there are double piscinas in each transept, with intersecting round arches, and carefully interwoven mouldings form part of a dado of blank arcading. The intersecting arches form points and it was thought that this was the origin of the Gothic pointed arch, a theory now discredited, for, as suggested in Chapter 1, it seems likely that the origins are more complex. Other

Cambridgeshire items are the ten Early English towers, an unusually large number. The finest are those at Bottisham and at Leverington; the latter is a composition, with spire, of all styles, but is entirely Early English up to the bell-openings stage. Above the west doorway is a gable with a small trefoiled niche for a statue, the windows are lancets and there are large polygonal buttresses. Bourn, has a west doorway of six orders.

Spires. Norfolk and Suffolk are chiefly remarkable for their glorious wool churches in the Perpendicular style and, therefore, have few notable spires. Cambridgeshire, on the other hand, has much from the earlier periods and Lincolnshire is generally regarded as the best county in England for the Decorated period. As a result there is a regional division between the frequency of spires in the purely East Anglian part and the two counties adjoining.

The prevalence of good stone spires is dependent upon the wealth of an area at the time when spires were the natural accompaniment to the current Decorated style. This was the case where weaving was practised in the fourteenth century, and is the reason why they are so frequent in the area between Gloucestershire and south Lincolnshire, this also coincided with the regions where the best limestone was available, especially in an area twenty to thirty miles east of a line drawn from Newark, Nottinghamshire, to Northampton. Spires tend to be localized where good stone occurs along with economic well-being, and it is noticeable that, in Cambridgeshire, they die out east of the river Cam. It is in the part bordering on Northamptonshire that they are most frequent. They occur at Willingham and Over, but the best is at Whittlesey, which is a late example, having been built about the middle of the fifteenth century. It is crocketed, and connected with the tower by flying buttresses linking with the pinnacles on the corners of the tower – a splendid, uplifting sight. Curious, rather than beautiful, is the twisted lead-sheathed timber spire at Bourn.

It is difficult not to overdo the superlatives when writing about Lincolnshire. Nevertheless, as already mentioned, this county can well claim the crown for Decorated churches, so it is only to be expected that many arresting spires will be found, among them some of the tallest in England.

As already mentioned, the broach was a discovery of the thirteenth century, while the recessed parapet type came in the fourteenth century. Generally, the spire-lights needed for ventilation are on the cardinal faces, but sometimes on the alternate ones. Many are crocketed. Spires are more frequent in Kesteven and Holland than in Lindsey. The finest of the broach type are at St Mary, Stamford, Ewerby and Frampton, and of the recessed parapet form there are examples at Grantham, Claypole, Moulton, Osberton and Louth, which is the loveliest of all.

Long Sutton is one of the earliest lead spires in England. It is 162 feet high and is placed on top of the early thirteenth-century tower. The whole looks tilted and this effect is accentuated by the inward-leaning lead spirelets which terminate the tower buttresses.

Decorated. As Pevsner writes, 'for the Decorated style Lincolnshire is the best county of all'. There are no qualifications, except later when he points out that the interiors often disappoint 'a little after the external displays'. The reason for this may be that the county had few rich land-owners and the prosperous farmers may not have been interested to the same extent. This would also account for the sparsity of good roofs and screens, which cannot be compared, except perhaps for two churches in Stamford, with those of Norfolk and Suffolk.

Externally, however, there is a feast and the interiors are far from being without interest. Two of the most enjoyable items are the south porch and the chancel furnishings of Heckington. The latter includes a superb Easter Sepulchre. The porch has large projecting buttresses with spacious canopied niches for statues, sadly, long since gone; above the arch is a pointed gable, the space between being filled with a wavy band, which encloses the figure of a seated Christ at the apex and angels and shields lower down. The Easter Sepulchre, one of a small group in this part of England which includes Hawton in Nottinghamshire, is divided into richly carved panels of the finest craftsmanship. The other furnishings in the chancel are a piscina, carved sedilia and a tomb recess containing a monument to Richard de Potesgrave, chaplain to Edward III, who is said to have rebuilt the chancel.

Heckington is the high point in a group which includes Sleaford, Holbeach, Gedney (pl. 43), Claypole, Boston and the south chapel of Grantham. Boston's interior, one of the most spacious in England, reflects the opulence bred of maritime trade. Not far behind is Helpringham.

No survey of the Decorated style in Lincolnshire would, however, be complete without a reference to window tracery. Here we find inexhaustible permutations and combinations of flowing designs in window decoration, culminating in the thrill of the Bishop's Eye window in Lincoln Cathedral. But to see the most exciting patterns one should go to the churches already mentioned – Heckington, Sleaford and Grantham – and the east windows of Boothby Pagnell in Kesteven and Haltham-on-Bain in Lindsey.

Cambridgeshire is also a notable Decorated county. The early fourteenth century was a golden period for church architecture there, particularly at Ely. The ogee curve began to appear at Swavesey, Willingham and Trumpington. This last, and St Mary the Less at Cambridge are the main examples of smaller Decorated churches in the county. Swavesey is built of a buff stone and presents a noble aspect from the south. So, too, does Willingham, but the material is brown rubble. Otherwise, at Willingham, the main Decorated features are the tower with broaches and spire, and the chancel. Although this was reconstructed at the end of the nineteenth century not too much harm was done. Especially large transomed windows, which are a feature of the style in Cambridgeshire, can be seen at Fen Ditton, Isleham and Rampton. The tracery is inventive and interesting, but fine as the tracery is, it is not up to Lincolnshire's standard.

Sutton is six miles from Ely, the influence of which is immediately apparent in the octagonal top of the tower, undoubtedly derived from the cathedral's magnificent lantern. Approaching from the south, a hill rises sharply from the lowlying fen country – one of the elevated sites where the population collected in this once flooded land. Presiding over the community and standing out against the rather modest houses of yellow brick below, is one of the most interesting churches in the county. It was built at the end of Edward III's reign, when Decorated was giving way to Perpendicular and here the process can be followed, for instance, in the east window. The interior is free from later tampering and shows the local feature of tall blank arcading along the chancel and aisle walls. (Wilburton and Histon are other examples of this.) The crowning delight, however, is the tower. This is faced with Barnack stone and surmounted by two battlemented octagons, using broaches to bridge the transition between square and lower octagon, and finished off with pinnacles, a spectacular apex to the pyramid of village and hill and a landmark for miles around.

Norfolk's major Decorated church is Snettisham with tower and tall spire rising to 176 feet. Spire-lights are used sparingly and flying buttresses link it to the tower pinnacles in the Louth and Whittlesey fashion. It has lost its chancel, and the tower, instead of being a crossing tower, rests rather heavily at the east end of the nave. The west window is a startling piece of six lights and very elaborate tracery. Spacious chancels and naves are a feature of this county's churches. At Winterton, East Tuddenham, Tittleshall and Bunwell they are over thirty feet wide and Elsing, though aisleless, is forty feet wide.

Other buildings to note are Great Walsingham and Hingham, built by the rector between 1319 and 1359, and the chancel of South Lopham. At Elsing there is an outstanding brass, perhaps one of the finest in the country, to Sir Hugh Hastings, the builder of the church.

Suffolk has little from the Decorated period; spires are rare and perhaps the only feature worthy of mention is the wooden porch at Boxford, which may be the earliest in the country. This scarcity, however, only makes what is to come the more dramatic, for we are in one of the greatest of the wool counties. Before leaving the fourteenth century, the gatehouses of Bury St Edmunds Abbey and of Butley Priory must be mentioned, for here are some of the earliest examples of flushwork, the mixing of knapped flint and stone to produce patterns. Despite the hardness of flint, the skilled knapper could split it into two fairly easily, and the inside of the stone was then faced outwards to produce a uniformly shaped material which is combined with ordinary freestone. This was used to a great extent in the absence of good stone and softens the otherwise unsympathetic texture which unrelieved flint produces.

Stone. Flushwork arose out of the necessity to make the most of what is available and, so far as building materials in Norfolk and Suffolk are concerned, this is not very much. Where the substratum is not chalk, as in parts of west Norfolk, there are only silts and clays, so that flints, either embedded in the chalk or washed out to form round pebbles and cobbles, are the main materials for all but the more important churches. There is, however, in the area around Sandringham, a narrow strip of older formations which produce the gritty, rather soft dark-brown sandstone called carstone, akin to wealden sandstones. Its colour has given it the name 'gingerbread' stone and it is a warm if not very durable material. The more important buildings could rely upon good water transport to bring in oolitic limestones, such as Ancaster, Ketton and Barnack, from the neighbouring counties, and these are used for the great marshland churches, the tower of Beccles in Suffolk and the cathedrals of Norwich and Ely.

In comparison, Lincolnshire is rich indeed. In the south-west occurs Ancaster, one of the best oolitic limestones. It is to this stone, and the other easily transported limestones, that so much of the elegance and grace of the marshland churches are due. There are many other lesser materials, including Spilsby sandstone in the Wolds, and one of the characteristics of the county is the varied colours of the stones used. Not unnaturally, in a county so well endowed with stone, timber is conspicuous by its absence, but brick is found and the keep of Tattershall Castle is one of the best examples of the early use of this material.

Cambridgeshire is one-third chalk, two-thirds fen. Clunch, the harder variety of chalk, is often used but, for the more imposing buildings, stone was brought in from Barnack in Northamptonshire; the county, however, has no great rivers and the scope for doing this was therefore limited. (Now, of course, due to the 1965 changes, Barnack is in Huntingdonshire.)

Wealth. In the past, the Church and the nobility were the main patrons of parish churches. By the end of the Middle Ages, the power of the former was waning because, like the rest of the population, the monasteries and the priesthood had been decimated by the Black Death, and the nobles were doing their best to destroy themselves in the Lancastrian/Yorkist power struggles. The Wars of the Roses (1455–85), were largely family rivalries, and affected the general life of the people very little. The wars did not stop the growth of the new capitalist class who were making fortunes from sheep-rearing and weaving. Previously weaving had largely been a cottage industry, but now it became concentrated into fewer hands. These merchants were anxious to beautify their home towns, and perhaps perpetuate their own memories, and nowhere could this be better done than in the focal point of the whole community – the parish church. They naturally built themselves beautiful homes, Great Chalfield Manor in Wiltshire is one, but these tend to be overshadowed by the grander residences that went up in Tudor, Stuart and Georgian times. Many of the churches, on the other hand, still remain, to make us admire the confident assurance with which they were built.

The civic pride of the rising middle class was shown in towers and perhaps porches, while personal pride was reflected in monuments, chantries, altars or aisles, for example, the Clopton chantry at Long Melford. We must be grateful that these able men were sufficiently God-fearing to devote so much of their money to this purpose in an age when masons were so well equipped to produce great works. There are certain parts of England where these benefactions are more noticeable than anywhere else and this is certainly one of them.

Perpendicular. It is a human predilection to want to pick the best of anything, whether it be man-made or natural. An attempt to do this for Norfolk churches has been made by G. W. D. Winkley, editor of the *Diocesan Directory*, in the excellent booklet *Norfolk Country Churches and the Future*, published by the Norfolk Society. This excludes Norwich and King's Lynn. His 'prize' list contains twelve names and they include All Saints at Walsoken, St Mary at West Walton (pl. 37) and Walpole St Peter (pl. 38). The first two have been mentioned, it is now St Peter's turn.

This church, which could claim to be the finest village church in England, was built between 1350 and 1400 and therefore is a transitional late Decorated/early Perpendicular building. What is particularly significant is that the three churches – one Norman, one Early English and one late Decorated/early Perpendicular – are not more than five miles apart one from the other, and it must be rare to be able to see so many mediaeval styles at their best in parish churches within such a small compass. This marshland area also includes Terrington St Clement, a Perpendicular building also in Mr Winkley's 'top twelve', as well as Wiggenhall St Mary the Virgin and Wiggenhall St Germans which have the most complete sets of early sixteenth-century benches in the county.

This is one tiny, remote corner of Norfolk. In the rest of the county the churches at Salle and Cawston are outstanding. Salle certainly qualifies as one of England's best twelve and Cawston has one of the finest roofs (pl. 41). Elsewhere in this region Suffolk has a stately group of churches in the north-east – Southwold (pl. 36), Blythburgh and Walberswick – and another in the south – Long Melford (pl. 33), Lavenham (pl. 32), Cavendish, Clare and Sudbury's churches. Lincolnshire has superb buildings in the south-west marshland area – Gedney (pl. 43), the Stamford churches, Quadring and Boston – not to mention the north-eastern group of Louth, Theddlethorpe All Saints and Addlethorpe.

It is impossible with such an *embarras de richesse* to do more than point the way. It is clear that the marshland, whether in Lincolnshire or Norfolk, was the source of great wealth and that this stemmed from the sheep which thrived on the grazing. Lincolnshire had the right stone and north-west Norfolk could get it, so that here was the perfect blend of wealth and materials. Salle and Cawston were built of imported stone, Salle of Barnack and Cawston partially, it is believed, of Caen stone which was transported by sea to Coltishall and thence overland. The money for Salle came from more than one wool family – the Boleyns, ancestors of Anne, the Fountaines and the Briggs, who also provided for chantry chapels. The village sign of Cawston has, as a central figure, a weaver at his loom and the church is dedicated to St Agnes, the patron saint of weavers. But the mainspring for its building was, for this period, exceptionally aristocratic, for its glory owes much to Sir Michael de la Pole, Earl of Suffolk and his wife, Catherine. Norwich and King's Lynn, as the most important mediaeval towns, do not lag behind. St Nicholas, King's Lynn and St Peter Mancroft, Norwich are the most notable churches.

The further one travels from the limestone belt, the more flint is used. Suffolk churches are built of flint. This might be considered a disadvantage, but anyone who has seen Southwold (pl. 36), Blythburgh, Lavenham (pl. 32) and Long Melford (pl. 33) will find that the obstacle has been more than magnificently overcome. Long Melford, although perhaps not typical of a Suffolk parish church, is of well-nigh cathedral proportions, sited so splendidly above the village and viewed so well from the green. Eighteen clerestory windows above twelve main windows on each side create the perfect glasshouse effect at which Perpendicular designers aimed and, from the south, we can see flush-work at its most effective. The money behind this came from the Clopton family and the outstanding monument is the Clopton chantry, dating from about 1500, which is an extension to the east chapel, formerly the Clopton chapel, of the north aisle. Clopton memorials abound both as brasses or monuments.

The impetus behind Lavenham, five miles away, came from the Springs and Branches, wealthy clothiers, although the Lord of the

Manor, John de Vere, Earl of Oxford also played a part. Later, a Spring married a de Vere, and the two sources of wealth were merged. Pevsner has commented that Lavenham 'is as interesting historically as it is rewarding architecturally. In both respects it is a match for Long Melford. The nave of Melford may be the nobler design, but Lavenham has more unity.' The tower, 140 feet high, is much larger than that of Long Melford and without pinnacles, but the church is, none the less, spectacular, especially when seen for the first time.

Why, one may ask, were such huge churches built for populations which may not have been able to fill them even in those times? The answer is well put in the guide to Walpole St Peter, 'Men built an immense church to the greater glory of God, who is immense. The whole church is a great offering of beauty to God.' What more can be said, except that today we might bear this in mind when considering whether a church is redundant because of the smallness of the congregation.

Suffolk is so rich in its churches that it is difficult to mention every one. However, Mildenhall and the two Bury St Edmunds buildings, one of which is now elevated to cathedral status, are very fine and worth visiting. Suffolk's porches must also be mentioned. Lavenham has a famous one, but possibly the best are at Woolpit and Beccles. The latter is, itself, a notable Perpendicular church with a fine separate tower. These porches are richly ornamented and many have upper storeys. Mildenhall has one such which was open to the church and used as a Lady Chapel. Porches played a far more important part in village life in mediaeval times than they do today. The initial stages of the baptismal service, churching of women (thanksgiving for safe childbirth) and of marriage were conducted in the porch. It was also used in the great procession on Palm Sunday, and sometimes, as at Weston-in-Gordano, Somerset, a temporary gallery was erected for singers who threw palm branches down before the processionists. Bargains were made and sworn in the porch. It was used for legal transactions and other business. The upper rooms were the local strong-room and there may even have been a custodian there with a window looking out on to the church. At Cirencester, Gloucestershire, a three-storeyed porch was for a long time used as the town hall. Other examples of fine porches in the eastern lowlands are Kersey, Eye and Southwold in Suffolk; St Nicholas, King's Lynn and Pulham St Mary the Virgin in Norfolk and Addlethorpe in Lincolnshire. The finest of all may be

Northleach in Gloucestershire, but these East Anglian examples make an impressive group.

Lincolnshire Perpendicular, with the exception of Louth, is not quite up to Lincolnshire Decorated and the outstanding examples fall a little short of those in Norfolk and Suffolk. Tattershall (pl. 42), however, shows the glasshouse ideal carried out as well as anywhere and is a complete example built entirely, at the instigation of Lord Cromwell, of Ancaster stone during the Wars of the Roses in the middle of the fifteenth century. The interior is rather lacking in decoration.

Louth is another of the unforgettable churches of England, not only for its wonderful tower and spire but also for its spacious and beautifully proportioned interior. It is the glory of Lindsey.

Theddlethorpe All Saints and Addlethorpe, which have already been mentioned, fall into this period. Coming south from Lindsey into Kesteven and Holland, many churches were altered during the Perpendicular period, especially at Stamford which had been in the wars. Interestingly, the steeple at All Saints was paid for by Calais merchants. Grantham and Gedney were also altered. The latter had a magnificent clerestory (pl. 43) added. But Lincolnshire churches do not show the complete rebuildings found elsewhere.

Cambridgeshire, which has no pronounced local style in its churches, shows the influences of its neighbouring counties. The Cambridgeshire representatives are, with the possible exception of Great St Mary, Cambridge, not quite up to the level of, say, Saffron Walden.

Among village churches, Burwell is an impressive example. It was completely rebuilt between 1460 and 1520, an undertaking financed by the Bernt family. It is the finest Perpendicular church in the county, and is typical in the number of windows, the tall slender columns and the feeling of space. There is much use of panelled tracery and, above the chancel arch, a wheel-window, but one without spokes. The building material is flint rubble, and externally the building is embattled. With fan-tracery in the north porch and a fine roof, it only needs an imposing tower to complete the effect and this it has. It is crowned with an open lantern, obviously inspired by Ely.

There are fine chancels at Swavesey, Orwell and Over, and the nave at Horseheath is noteworthy.

Towers. With all its other virtues, the towers of this area are not in the same class as other parts of the churches. Starting with Cambridge-shire, we find towers that share East Anglian, Northamptonshire and Hertfordshire characteristics. A distinctive local trait is the employ-ment of octagonal turrets which may have been derived from Ely. Elm, an Early English tower, has this feature. It is seen to best advantage, however, at Haslingfield (pl. 31), but the use of clunch, which deteriorates, necessitated resurfacing in the nineteenth century. Octagonal tops, another local feature, occur at St Cyriac, Swaffham Prior and, in a double form, at Sutton. But, sadly, St Cyriac is in a dilapidated state. Paired windows, derived from Northamptonshire, add much to the dignity of Swavesey and Guilden Morden, which is further enhanced by pinnacles. Wisbech is a late and curious hybrid with an elaborate, sharply stepped parapet. Many have leaded spirelets of Hertfordshire type.

Norfolk and Suffolk towers can be taken together and form a local style not found elsewhere. They are nearly all of flint, which precludes carving and is difficult at corners, so that stone dressings have to be used, giving a rather skimped effect. Terrington St Clement, Cawston, and the north-west tower of St Margaret's, King's Lynn, however, are of oolite. Instead of carved decoration much use is made of flushwork, and the whole of the west face of Redenhall in Norfolk and of Eye and Laxfield in Suffolk are covered in this manner. The absence of parapets and pinnacles gives an unfinished look to many of them and it is curious why pinnacles, a small item in relation to the total cost, were omitted. Professor Allen thinks that a spire may have been intended which never materialized. As there are about one thousand towers, few can be mentioned, but Salle and Cromer should be singled out. The latter has parapet and pinnacles and, at 159 feet, is the tallest in East Anglia. Salle in Professor Allen's opinion, is one of the best compositions in Norfolk.

Buttresses frequently terminate at the lower stages of the belfry storey and, in Norfolk, practically no stair-turret continues above the top. Instead they stop short and finish well below.

The best of the Suffolk towers is probably Eye with clasping, octagonal buttresses ending in pinnacles, but there is rather too much emphasis on the horizontal courses. Eye and Bungay are striking, and Lavenham and Beccles have already been mentioned. Individual towers of con-siderable appeal are Stoke-by-Nayland and Mendlesham, which has ornament concentrated on the skyline where it is most effective. Stoke has extremely prominent buttresses. The impact is greatly increased as it is situated on the ridge of a hill and can be seen for miles around.

Lincolnshire towers are not of the first water, but there is a group in and around Stamford which has pinnacles and paired windows under an arch bisected by a mullion. The best of these is at Folkingham. Another is a late Perpendicular one at Great Ponton, with its odd weather-vane in the shape of a viol. Other good towers are at Pinchbeck, which leans, and Coningsby, plain but well mannered. Another group with ogee-headed windows in the top stage includes Tetney, Beckingham and Sedgebrook. Boston, which took over two hundred years to complete, is a law unto itself and the people who built it seem to have sacrificed quality for one-upmanship. The lower stages have very shallow blind panelling decoration but the lantern, which is completely open, is a more graceful feature.

Roofs. Shortage of stone is often partially compensated for by an abundance of good timber. The carpenters of East Anglia turned this to glorious account in their roofs. Throughout the Middle Ages, workers in wood sought to improve their efficiency and the beauty of their products. To increase strength, upright posts were inserted between tie-beams and steeply pitched roofs – kingposts if only one, queenposts if two. Out of this development arose the hammer-beam form, an ingenious method of narrowing the span by throwing out two short beams from the walls, bracing these and placing an upright post at the ends of the beams. This might be done again further up, in which case a double hammer-beam was formed. These are the peaks of timber-roof construction, functionally sound and aesthetically very satisfying as they draw the eye upward.

The roofs are open and dispense with the tie-beam, and are embellished with much elaborate carving, particularly figures of angels with wings outstretched. Some of the finest of these roofs are situated in and around London – Westminster Hall, an early one of the fourteenth century; Crosby Hall, Chelsea; Eltham Palace and, possibly the most elaborate of them all, the Great Hall at Hampton Court Palace. But, in parish churches, the type reached perfection in Norfolk and Suffolk, and at March in Cambridgeshire.

The ordinary Norfolk roofs are bolder than most in that they sometimes dispense with a collar; they are refined and dignified. Suffolk roofs are more notable, in that they are richer in detail. Of the fourteen Norfolk and twenty Suffolk examples of hammer-beam roofs, one must mention the single hammer-beam roof at Cawston (pl. 41) and the double ones at Gissing, Knapton, Tilney All Saints and Swaffham in Norfolk; the single at Earl Stonham, Badingham and Hopton and double at Grundisburgh, Woolpit and Worlingworth in Suffolk. March in Cambridgeshire has been mentioned, other double hammer-beams in that county are at Elm and Willingham; Bourn has a single one. The majority, however, are of flatter type. Apart from the four in Essex nowhere else can these exceptional roofs be found. Even in Lincolnshire, so well favoured in other respects, the roofs fall far short of East Anglian standards, Stamford's St John and St Mary being the best.

Screens. Further fields for the skills of the wood-carver were the rood-screens. These screens supported roods, representations of Christ on the Cross attended by the Virgin Mary and St John the Evangelist, and became the focal point of mediaeval churches. It is not to be wondered at, therefore, that the craftsman lavished his utmost skill on this central feature.

The screens of East Anglia are quite outstanding. As in Somerset and Devonshire, a type was evolved in which the top of the screen is fanned out into projecting vaults which supported the rood-loft. East Anglian screens, in general, differ from those in the other two counties in being loftier and lighter, in keeping with the architecture, and in having better-painted figures in the panels at the base.

H. Munro Cautley, the great expert on East Anglian churches, states that over two hundred Norfolk churches have screens or parts of them and the majority are fifteenth century, as they are in Suffolk. Pevsner comments that 'they cannot compete with Devonshire in richness of decoration, but they are in their greater restraint just as impressive'. Attleborough (pl. 40) in Norfolk and Eye in Suffolk, now restored to its former glory, are outstanding among the area's riches. The painted screen panels of East Anglia are of great beauty, the Twelve Apostles being the favourite subject. The finest series is at Ranworth and others are at Barton Turf, Ludham, Cawston, Beeston Regis, Hunstanton and Carleton Rode in Norfolk, and Southwold, Eye,

Westhall and Somerleyton in Suffolk. Gesso work is often used in Suffolk.

Guilden Morden and Balsham, with its vaulting, are the best in Cambridgeshire. In Lincolnshire the wood-work is not in the same class, but Addlethorpe's screen is typical.

Fonts. The remaining Norman Tournai marble fonts are at Lincoln Cathedral and at Thornton Curtis in Lincolnshire, and at St Peter, Ipswich, with a fragment in Christchurch Museum in the same town. Barnetby in Lincolnshire may justly claim to possess the best lead font in England. East Anglian fonts are often raised on traceried steps which add to their dignity, for example, Little Walsingham, Norfolk and Laxfield, Suffolk.

The characteristic font of East Anglia is, however, the octagonal type which became general in the fifteenth century but which, in the Seven Sacraments' form, is unique to this part of England, except for Farningham, Kent and Nettlecombe, Somerset.

The Seven Sacrament fonts show the sacraments of Baptism, Confirmation, Mass, Penance, Holy Orders, Holy Matrimony and Extreme Unction with, usually, the Crucifixion or the Baptism of Christ on the eighth side. There are twenty-two in Norfolk and eleven in Suffolk. Gresham, Walsoken and Sloley in Norfolk and Badingham in Suffolk are the best preserved.

The other octagonal type shows the emblems of the Evangelists plus four figures of angels or demi-figures bearing shields with coats of arms or emblems of the Passion or Trinity. The bowl is often supported by angels and around the pedestal are four seated lions and sometimes four wild men, representing the mediaeval concept of sin subdued by baptism.

Norfolk has all types and periods of font but, apart from one brick one at Potter Heigham and one lead one at Brundall, all are of stone. There is an outstanding group of Norman fonts in north-west Norfolk, at Shernborne, South Wootton, Burnham Deepdale and Fincham.

The remaining two completely enveloping font canopies must also be mentioned. These are at Trunch and St Peter Mancroft, Norwich. The finest font cover, of any period, in the country is at Ufford, Suffolk.

After this, one can pass over Cambridgeshire, but South Ormsby and Huttoft in Lincolnshire have elaborate Perpendicular examples.

Other furnishings. Space prevents further detailed summaries of the wealth of furnishings in this area, but the bench-ends of Norfolk and Suffolk deserve a brief reference. The commonest type here end in a finial, called a 'poppy-head', instead of the square-headed type common elsewhere, and some have little figures beside the poppy-heads. One of the most delightful examples of the latter is at Blythburgh where the Seven Deadly Sins are portrayed, with Sloth sitting up in bed. Complete sets of mediaeval benches are very rare, but Fressingfield in Suffolk has one; in Norfolk, the most complete are at Wiggenhall St Mary the Virgin, Wiggenhall St Germans and Great Walsingham. The best set in Lincolnshire is at Osbournby and in Cambridgeshire at Swavesey and Isleham.

The east windows of St Peter Mancroft, Norwich, and East Harling, Norfolk, are filled with lovely mediaeval glass. Other churches to visit for this feature are Leverington and Wimpole, Cambridgeshire and Combs in Suffolk.

This is an area rich in good brasses, but they are too numerous to list. St Gregory's, Norwich, has a captivating brass door-knocker hidden away behind a curtain. The famous painted retable at Thornham Parva in Suffolk has even been exhibited in Paris.

A word must be added on monuments. This being a field for the stone-carver, Lincolnshire comes back into the picture with the best examples. The other three counties have very little to offer, but Lincolnshire is rich in stone sculpture, so far as England can be after the depredations of the Reformation. St Mary, Stamford, has a female figure dating from 1380 which is especially beautiful.

General. The gently rolling country of south Cambridgeshire and the valleys of the Lincolnshire Wolds are some of the most appealing parts of this lowlying land. From a landscape point of view one might call it uneventful, but for those interested in churches it is doubtful whether one can find any other area so exciting and so varied. The wealth brought by wool overcame magnificently the shortage of stone in Norfolk and Suffolk and, where both were combined, as in Lincolnshire, the resultant architectural achievement is quite breathtaking. The county could claim to have the finest church of all – Lincoln Cathedral – and, even if one were to dispute this, it is hard to argue with Louth's claim to have the finest tower/spire group in the country. Heckington is a masterpiece of

84

the Decorated style and Grantham of more than one style. One may have reservations about the artistic quality of Boston Stump, but it cannot be denied that it is the tallest tower in the land – anything less stumpish it would be difficult to imagine!

The Norfolk wool churches and the many glorious buildings in Suffolk are hard to match anywhere and what they lost in stone they made up for in wood. Cambridgeshire, too, although not quite in the same category, partakes of East Anglian splendour and is a link between the East and the next region – the Midlands.

East Riding magnificence, Somerset towers, Gloucestershire splendour, Herefordshire Norman and Devonshire screens are still to come, but England's eastern lowlands are one of the richest areas for parish churches. The tide of prosperity has receded today and there are many ruins to witness to this. The sea, too, has swept away much of the unstable glacial deposits which formed the coast, but which had no firm foundation to provide support. Some churches, like Dunwich, have disappeared altogether. With 659 mediaeval churches in Norfolk alone, maintaining them, quite apart from holding services in all of them, is a major problem. Some now serve other purposes, such as museums, for example St Peter Hungate, Norwich. But whatever their use, whatever part of the area one is in, there are glorious examples of parish church architecture.

7 EASTERN MIDLANDS

Much of the area of the eastern Midlands once formed part of Middle Anglia, one of the kingdoms of the Saxon Heptarchy. Later it was absorbed into Mercia which, under its great King Offa, reached its zenith in the eighth century.

After the death of St Augustine, the Gospel was spread through the land by two main streams. One travelled northwards along the eastern side of the country; carried by St Augustine's successors, especially St Paulinus, it reflected Roman influences. The other came south down the west side and was carried by St Aidan's successors, notably St Chad and St Wulstan. This stream of Christianity had Celtic influences.

Mercia, however, was not won over to Christianity until the middle of the seventh century and, once again, it was a woman of royal blood who paved the way. Paeda, son of Penda the last heathen King of Mercia, was to marry Elchfrida, daughter of the King of Northumbria, and one of the conditions of the marriage was that the princess should be able to practise and spread her own religion. This was agreed, and she brought with her to Hrewpandun (now Repton), the Mercian capital, four Irish priests named Adda, Betti, Cedd and Diuma, the last of whom was to become the first bishop of the Mercians. Initially, therefore, the impulse for conversion came from the Celtic side, but later the Romans took over.

Anglo-Saxon. It is hard to believe today that the small town of Repton was once the capital of a kingdom. Be that as it may the crypt of the tenth-century church still remains below the chancel of the present church, with the rare dedication to St Wystan. The crypt's rough groined vaults are supported on four columns which have the uncommon decoration of spiral bands running up the shafts.

The east Midlands retain more pre-Conquest work than any other part of England. The most considerable building of this era is Brixworth church near Northampton which, as noted in Chapter 1, was described by Clapham as 'perhaps the most imposing architectural memorial of the seventh century surviving north of the Alps'. Whether what now remains is of the seventh century or tenth century cannot be stated with certainty, but it is known that the original building was of the Roman type with an apse and that it had clerestories and aisles as well. Although the aisles have now disappeared, its dimensions are larger than any other Anglo-Saxon church in England. One can still see the solid pillars of the nave and the arches above, made of Roman bricks. Externally, the tower with its staircase to the west is a prominent feature. This was heightened in the fourteenth century when a spire was added. The visual pleasure of the whole church is greatly enhanced by the warm brown ironstone of which it is built (pl. 50).

Great Paxton, in Huntingdonshire, is another major Anglo-Saxon building. It has a true crossing and proper piers instead of the lumps of walling at Brixworth. This church was once a Saxon minster, that is, a church which was monastic and sent out missionaries to spread the message of Christianity. The exterior has a mainly Perpendicular appearance, and gives little hint of the earlier interior.

Barnack, the home of the famous mediaeval oolite quarry, also has Saxon work of great interest. The tower up to the bell-openings stage dates from about 1000 and is decorated with pilaster strips and the familiar long-and-short quoins. In addition, in the tower, there are stone slabs with interlacing ornaments surmounted by a carved bird, and triangular-headed openings. Inside, the tower opens into the nave through an imposing arch, nearly twenty feet high, and with imposts like huge stone sandwiches. Also at Barnack, an outstanding carved effigy of Christ, three feet three inches high, was found under the floor of the north aisle in 1931. Artistically, the draperies and the expression are of the highest order and the whole piece is magnificently executed. The bearded figure of Christ is seated, holding a book in the left hand and with the right hand raised in benediction. At the back of the head is a nimbus and the whole is enclosed in a frame of stone. This must be one of the noblest survivals of pre-Conquest sculpture in the country and it is significant that it was discarded, presumably by the Normans, as an ordinary piece of rubble, no doubt in an attempt to discredit anything Saxon.

The fame of the Barnack tower is matched, if not exceeded, by the one at Earls Barton which has recently celebrated its millennium. Apart from the battlements at the top, the whole of it is Saxon and it is even more elaborately decorated. Pilaster strips, possibly based on timber motifs, are used vertically, diagonally and in X-patterns, and the bell-openings have no less than five arches divided by baluster shafts. The effect is, however, marred by the cement rendering which has been used to cover the walls. A third tower of interest is Brigstock, which has a western staircase projection like Brixworth.

Wittering, only three miles from Barnack, has another forceful chancel arch, with roll mouldings and crude capitals looking like great slabs of cheese. The effect is accentuated because it is next to a post-Conquest mid-twelfth-century nave arcade with scalloped capitals and arches decorated with zigzag and lozenge ornaments. The unpolished Saxon work makes even the restrained Norman look sophisticated by comparison. In Northamptonshire, Little Billing has a Saxon font.

Two other pieces of carving, both dating from about 800, must be mentioned. At Breedon-on-the-Hill in Leicestershire, thirty fragments, mostly in the form of friezes, remain from a carving of this time. They are in a variety of forms and different styles of most unusual type. At Wirksworth, Derbyshire, a stone was found below the surface when the pavement in front of the altar was being removed in 1820. It lay over a stone-built vault containing a large and perfect human skeleton. The stone is decorated with various scenes, including some from the life of Christ, which run into one another and have crowded, dumpy figures in a rather rustic style. There are some doubts as to its true nature but, because of where it was found, it is often referred to as a coffin lid. It is now affixed to the wall of the north aisle.

The crosses, erected for various purposes in the churchyards, are a legacy of the Mercian phase of Christianity in this region. One of the finest of these is at Eyam, in Derbyshire. It is complete except for the top part of the shaft. Eyam was struck by the plague in 1665, and condemned itself to heroic isolation in order to avoid spreading the dreaded scourge to neighbouring places. It thus increased the risks of infection enormously and through this great act of self-denial lost about five-sixths of its population. The rector, William Mompesson, who proposed this drastic step, performed courageous ministry to the dying, among whom was his own wife.

The erection of crosses was brought to an end by the renewed invasions of the ninth century but was resumed, in a different style, in the tenth century. Stapleton, in Nottinghamshire, has a good example of these later crosses. Apart from this, the only other item in the county from this period is the base of Carlton-in-Lindrick's tower (pl. 54).

Norman. Perhaps nowhere is the severity of early Norman brought home more forcibly than in the nave of Blyth, in Nottinghamshire, originally a Benedictine priory. This sad remnant of the original aisled, cruciform building has been further obscured by the substitution of a Perpendicular tower for the old Norman one at the west end. Further mutilation has been caused by the removal of the last bay of the nave by the owners of nearby Blyth Hall to make room for an aviary.

Nottinghamshire's other major Norman building is at Worksop. This, too, was monastic, but shows a mixture of early and late Norman features. The former plainness is still evident in the west front but the long nave, with an unusual arrangement of tribune and clerestory above, is late, almost Transitional.

There were three Benedictine monasteries of importance – Peterborough (which became a cathedral in 1541), Thorney (once in Cambridgeshire) and Ramsey, Huntingdonshire – and their influence is felt at Castor, a remarkable Norman church with a splendid crossing tower. In the chancel there is an inscription in the shape of a tympanum, recording that the church was consecrated in 1124. The tower is a magnificent example of Norman decoration and must be one of the most interesting of this period in the country. The church is dedicated to St Kyneburga, who was the daughter of King Paeda and Queen Elchfrida, and foundress of Peterborough Abbey.

Northampton has two very impressive Norman churches, St Peter and Holy Sepulchre. There are good towers at Maxey (now Huntingdonshire) and Spratton. Leicester's two churches of this era, St Mary-de-Castro and St Nicholas, have been much Victorianized but the chancel of the former, which was lengthened about 1160, is a rich example of late Norman work and contains a piscina and sedilia of exceptionally beautiful design. St Nicholas has a good Norman tower.

Derbyshire has outstanding examples of a large parish church and a small village chapel. Melbourne, with its almost unique twin towers, is one of 'the most ambitious Norman parish churches of England' and contains a number of unusual features, including, on the north side, a wall-passage between clerestory windows and nave. The church has both aisles and transepts and the tall circular nave piers are four feet thick and so closely set together that the arches have to be stilted in order to accommodate them.

The village example, Steetley, is only just over fifty feet in length and is little more than a chapel. It is, however, more richly decorated than any other Norman church in the county. Unfortunately, the hand of the Victorian restorer is rather apparent.

At Tickencote, in Rutland, the late eighteenth-century restorers added a tower as well as making other structural alterations, but nothing can diminish the impact of the chancel arch (pl. 47), or the east front. Both are astonishingly luxurious but, as can be seen in the photo, the arch shows signs of faulty construction.

There is much else in this small county, which is one of the best for Norman work in the whole region. Morcott and Tixover are mainly twelfth-century village buildings with Norman west towers and Morcott has the rarity of an oculus window in the tower. Stoke Dry and Essendine have shafts and jambs carved all over with varying designs, another rarity. Essendine also has a fine tympanum, as have other Rutland churches, for example, Egleton.

Furnishings. Among the cream of the region's Norman furnishings are fonts, doorways and capitals.

The fonts at Waltham-on-the-Wolds in Leicestershire, Crick in Northamptonshire and the finely made lead font at Ashover, Derbyshire, which is only two feet across the bowl, are all well worth seeing. By far the best, however, and one of the finest Norman fonts in England, is the square, richly decorated font at Lenton, in Nottingham. Lenton is in a little-known part of the city and it is a delight to find such a treasure in so unexpected a place.

This region has some fine doorways. Among these are Balderton and Teversal in Nottinghamshire, St Mary-de-Castro in Leicester and Southoe in Huntingdonshire. Warboys, also in Huntingdonshire, has one of the bronze door-knockers which are so spirited and vigorous in their design.

Wakerley, in Northamptonshire has a remarkable pair of capitals on the chancel arch, one of which shows a siege with a castle and knights on horseback, wonderfully fitted into this restricted and awkward space. Although not very spiritual in feeling, it is astonishingly alive.

Early English. Although this region can boast no Early English architecture as impressive as Bedfordshire's Felmersham, there is, nevertheless, a great deal to see. In Rutland, particularly, it is possible to follow the gradual development from Norman to Gothic in considerable detail. The thirteenth century, too, was a good period in all the other counties in their different ways.

Many of the churches, however, were enlarged and altered in the following century so that complete Early English places of worship are infrequent. Among those that exist are Hannington, in Northamptonshire, with its tall, graceful pillars, and Etton, in the Soke of Peterborough. Both have great intrinsic beauty. Churches with good work of this period include Ashbourne and Chesterfield in Derbyshire, the Lady Chapel at Worksop in Nottinghamshire, Stoke Golding and Scalford in Leicestershire, Ketton (west front) in Rutland and Alconbury and Leighton Bromswold in Huntingdonshire. There are also many others. Special attention may be drawn to the south porch of Barnack church, which is not only very early but is also exceptionally fine.

Two local features which call for particular comment are the double piscinas of Huntingdonshire and the double bellcotes of Rutland. Double piscinas, which occur at Hemingford Grey, Houghton and St Ives, are placed under pointed arches with typical late thirteenth-century mouldings. Such piscinas had a very limited life because, towards the end of the century, a papal edict ordered that the rinsings of the chalice after administration of Holy Communion must be consumed by the officiating priests and not discarded down a drain. After this edict, single piscinas became the order of the day. Other examples of double piscinas, however, are found throughout the country.

The double bellcotes, with their supporting buttresses, are an engaging, rustic attribute of many a Rutland country church, for example, Manton, Essendine, Little Casterton among others. They make a charming contrast to the many stately towers and spires in this well-favoured county, and they also spill over into Leicestershire, for instance at Burton Lazars.

Towers and spires. Nowhere in England are there so many stone spires of all forms and types as in the east Midlands and south Lincolnshire. Northamptonshire is justly called 'the county of spires and squires' but Huntingdonshire and Rutland have many too, some small and rather dumpy but others tall and soaring, including Ketton (pl. 49), the ideal of so many Victorian architects. Derbyshire has its own brand, usually recessed behind battlements. It also has the notorious twisted one of lead at Chesterfield. Leicestershire, too, has some fine spires, and this feature only fades away in Nottinghamshire where, perversely, Newark has one of the best of all.

Why is it that there are so many in this region and the Kesteven area of Lincolnshire? Why do the other stone districts, Somerset, Gloucestershire and Dorset, not have as many? T. D. Atkinson supplies the answer. He points out that the spire area was comparatively wealthy in the thirteenth and fourteenth centuries when spires were the fashion. 'The land was favourable for the agriculture of the time, and the trade in wool was very large, Boston being by far the largest wool port. The prosperity of other regions – Yorkshire, Somerset, Gloucestershire, Norfolk and Suffolk – came when, in the latter part of the fourteenth century and in the fifteenth century, the wool was not exported as raw material, but as cloth', and at that time a tower without a spire was preferred.

The differences between the various types of spires have been outlined in Chapter 3. In general, the broach spire, whether with large or small broaches, preceded the parapet or recessed type, although there was an overlap between the two. Derbyshire tended towards the latter and the absence of ventilators or spire-lights, normally essential to prevent damp forming, is a local trait. West Huntingdonshire, on the other hand, is thick with broach spires, of which Spaldwick (pl. 45) is a good example. In Northamptonshire and Leicestershire, spire-lights, with some exceptions, are on the cardinal faces; in Rutland and Huntingdonshire the lowest and top tiers are on these faces, but the second tier is on the diagonal faces.

To select examples of broach spires in such a forest is invidious. Newark and Ketton have been mentioned. In Leicestershire, Market Harborough is a fine example. In Northamptonshire one can only indicate a few, such as Warmington and Raunds, but most of the finest are of the parapet type and would include Higham Ferrers, Rushden,

Oundle and Kettering, the last of which has crockets up the edges of the spire. Geddington and King's Sutton are others. Some, such as Higham Ferrers and Easton Maudit, have delicate flying buttresses connecting pinnacles and spire. King's Sutton has these between inner pinnacles and spire and also between outer and inner pinnacles. Bottesford in Leicestershire is of the parapet type.

Breadsall and Eckington, in Derbyshire, are chaste and graceful Early English examples and Bakewell (pl. 56) has a fourteenth-century spire on an octagon, rebuilt in the nineteenth century. Repton's spire, which is exceptional in having two tiers of dormer windows, rises to over two hundred feet and also dates from the fourteenth century, a worthy successor to the crossing tower of the tenth-century church.

However, many of the larger Derbyshire places of worship, such as Derby Cathedral, Tideswell (pl. 59) and Youlgreave, are without spires, and the region's towers must be considered. Some seem to stand out above all others. St Neot's in Huntingdonshire, All Saints in Derby (now the cathedral) and Titchmarsh in Northamptonshire are three such. As Professor Allen points out, it is the fenestration that counts, and he goes so far as to rate the tower of Titchmarsh as the finest parish church tower in England outside the Somerset group, although others would rate Chittlehampton in Devon and Probus in Cornwall higher. Other fine spireless towers in Northamptonshire are at Aldwincle All Saints and Whiston (pl. 55), a worthy accompaniment to a church built at the very end of the mediaeval period by Robert Catesby. Others in Huntingdonshire include Elton and St Mary, Huntingdon.

Leicestershire has many enjoyable towers, sometimes enhanced by unusual stone. Melton Mowbray and Loughborough, which can be grouped with St Mary's, Nottingham, are probably the finest. Not so well known are Sileby, Scalford and Stonesby, all of which are battlemented.

Rutland's main tower is of the fourteenth century at Whissendine, an uncommon design with deeply recessed west window and doorway.

Some east Midland towers are surmounted by an octagon, the inspiration for which may have come from the Ely octagon. Fotheringhay and Lowick in Northamptonshire are fine examples. In contrast, Hail Weston in Huntingdonshire has a timber tower which is more akin to those of Essex. There is another reminder of this county in the use of brick in the tower and porch at nearby Doddington.

Decorated. Early English often merges into Decorated in an imperceptible way with subtle changes in piers, capitals and especially window tracery. When Queen Eleanor's cortège passed through Northamptonshire in 1290, crosses were built at its temporary resting-places. To commemorate a member of the royal family only the best craftsmen were employed, which may have started the fashion in the county. The two finest crosses remaining from that time are Geddington and Hardingstone. At Cotterstock, a collegiate church, the magnificent chancel was begun in 1337, but the *pièce de résistance* of the Decorated period in this county is Finedon, built of a warm brown ironstone with grey stone dressings. This large and noble building enables one to study the style at its best. Byfield is mainly fourteenth century with a notable chancel and much ballflower, the favourite Decorated form of enrichment, in the splendid portal. Crick and Stanford, both mostly fourteenth century, are also fine. Stanford's glass, which dates from the first half of that century, is the finest in the county.

The fourteenth century is the high point for parish church architecture in Leicestershire, and Dr Hoskins has commented that 'into this period falls practically everything of the first class'. Wide aisles and sometimes aisled transepts occur, and some churches, for example Kegworth, have not been substantially altered since the fourteenth century.

With such abundance, it is impossible to mention everything. However, the exceptionally interesting church of Stoke Golding is full of delights, not least the capital with ladies wearing wimples and a youth sticking his tongue out. Kibworth Harcourt and Twycross have piers which flow into the arch in one continuous sweep without capitals. Kirby Bellars is shown in plate 48.

The main attractions in Rutland are the beautifully moulded arches in the nave of Whissendine, and the capitals both there and at Oakham. At Whissendine they are still stiff-leaf, but at Oakham they have developed into a different style. The exterior of Langham is another pleasure, as are the cluster of lovely sedilia, for example at North Luffenham.

Nottinghamshire and Derbyshire both profited from the benefactions of men of means and piety, a fact reflected in the beautifying and enlarging of chancels. Sometimes it was through the munificence of a bishop, for example Sandiacre; sometimes of an archdeacon as at

Chaddesden; but as in the case of Norbury, it was due to the lay rector or rector. The chancel of Woodborough, in Nottinghamshire, was the work of a de Strelley, and Hawton – 'one of the most exciting pieces of architecture in the county' – of Sir John de Compton. At Tideswell, 'the cathedral of the Peak' (pl. 59), the whole church was rebuilt in the fourteenth and fifteenth centuries, the chancel by John Foljambe.

Of furnishings, one must include the Easter Sepulchres of Hawton and Sibthorpe, Nottinghamshire. The former has all the laciness and exuberance of decoration of the Decorated phase and is the finest in the country. The stone screen at Ilkeston, Derbyshire, is a square-headed example of exquisite lightness and grace, and the wooden screen at Fenny Bentley in the same county has fan-tracery in the coving. A Derbyshire speciality, seen at Chaddesden and Taddington, is the provision of stone book-rests in the chancel walls.

In Huntingdonshire, too, chancels were made more splendid and it was again the lay rector who was responsible, between 1345 and 1352, for Fenstanton, the best of all. Perhaps the most extraordinary survival from this period is the polygonal apse at Bluntisham. It is a purely French style and exceedingly uncommon in England.

Economic situation. Economically, the region enjoyed a modest prosperity, helped by the Leicester breed of sheep, possibly common throughout the Midlands, which produced a grade of fine wool for export. In the fourteenth century the area's wealth was fairly widely spread, and had not yet started to accumulate in the hands of a relatively small number of capitalists. Weaving, which was one of the main sources of income in the fourteenth century, was largely a cottage industry. The emergence of great individual merchants, which led to the grand East Anglian churches, did not occur to anything like the same extent in the Midlands and so the Perpendicular period is not as strongly represented here.

Perpendicular. Only in Nottinghamshire is there an impression of greater things to come. The other counties of this region have good examples of fifteenth-century buildings, but one senses that the peak of mediaeval church architecture has been passed. Derbyshire is perhaps the poorest in this period, although Tideswell (pl. 59), one of the finest churches in the county, received a new and original tower. Northamptonshire has two splendid Perpendicular churches at Fotheringhay and Lowick. But even by the time Mary Queen of Scots met her fate at the castle, Fotheringhay had lost its chancel, and, although the nave is of East Anglian proportions, this former collegiate church, founded by a son of Edward III, is sadly mutilated. A feature of the county is the number of family chapels built in the sixteenth century, testifying to the fact that it is a county of squires as well as spires. At Oundle there is a particularly fine porch.

Leicestershire and Rutland fall away in this period except for towers. Huntingdonshire, however, has a complete Perpendicular church at St Neot's, which is nobly completed by its fine tower.

Furnishings, especially screens and roofs, do not compare with those of East Anglia and there is nothing of more than local importance.

Contrasting with the region's general paucity, Nottinghamshire can boast two major town churches of this period, of which Newark might well be included as one of England's top thirty churches. The other is St Mary, Nottingham. Newark is by no means all Perpendicular, but the general impression of the interior with its spacious nave and aisles is markedly fifteenth century. St Mary, almost entirely Perpendicular, is a noble monument to civic pride, although today it might seem a little dark. Nottinghamshire also has an exceptionally interesting village church at Holme-by-Newark, built by John Barton a wealthy merchant.

Building materials. Throughout this region good stone is either present or else not far away, and it certainly makes a change from the rough, unshaped flints of the previous region. Travelling west from the eastern lowlands, carstone, in the form of cobbles, appears in Huntingdonshire, and sometimes there is an agreeably buff-coloured rubble left over from oolite workings. Soon, however, it is the area of Barnack or Weldon oolite. Where stone was not available on the spot, it could be easily transported along the rivers Nene, Ouse and Welland.

Nottinghamshire has its own type of limestone, magnesian limestone, from the older formations. This magnesian form of the rock runs up in a thin band from just north of Nottingham, along the Nottinghamshire/Derbyshire border into Yorkshire and ends near Darlington, in County Durham. It is usually a light buff colour in Nottinghamshire. There are sandstones alongside, and these and the limestone are both quarried at Mansfield, Nottinghamshire. Rutland, too, has oolitic limestone quarries at Ketton, Clipsham and other places. There are, too, further good supplies just over the county boundary at Ancaster in Lincolnshire and Barnack in the Soke of Peterborough, together with a charming type of roofing slab from Collyweston nearby in Northamptonshire, which was to Cambridge what Stonesfield was to Oxford.

There is also marlstone and ironstone, the latter with its warm brown tones due to the presence of iron.

Northamptonshire has all this in profusion and was able to help other areas less well endowed.

Derbyshire has sandstone and, in the north, carboniferous limestone at the famous Hopton Wood quarries. In the north-east is the continuation of the belt of magnesian limestone from Nottinghamshire. Leicestershire had to make do with poorer materials. The county is a meeting-ground of old and young formations; there is even granite in the geologically complex Charnwood area. West is brick country, and only in the east was it possible to use local marlstone for building.

All this is reflected in the rich and varied colour of the east Midland churches: ranging from cool grey to warm orange with buffs and pinks in between. Sometimes purple infillings of limestone are to be seen in Leicestershire buildings, but these are building blocks, not building stone being used as such. In Derbyshire, the pinkish stone used so extensively tends to become darkened in industrial areas, making it rather sombre. This is strikingly brought home at Chesterfield where the church is being cleaned and once more the soft pinks beneath the grime can be seen.

General. The abiding impression of this area is the upward-reaching spire, symbolizing the soaring aspirations of a spiritual age and reflecting man's desire to reach up to God. The other main experience is the wonderful range of colour from the variety of building materials. Would that the interiors could still match the exteriors as they did before the wall-paintings were limewashed over and the stained glass smashed!

There is a just balance between the availability of good stone and the best scenery. Even ardent lovers of Northamptonshire would hardly claim that it is the most beautiful of English counties, but what wonderful use has been made of its noble oolite and its sunny ironstones in turning this material into lovely churches and villages. No wonder that it has attracted to itself many famous families who have lived in the same stately homes for centuries. One might argue that Rutland has the best of the bargain in that it is blessed both with stone and natural beauty and one can well understand its pride in its individual identity. Leicestershire, despite its rash of brick towards the west and rather dull industrial growth, has much unassuming charm and many signs of wool prosperity. One associates it, too, with good hunting country. Huntingdonshire is another county of quiet, unpretentious fascination with its lowlying, well-watered lands and its string of churches stretched out along the Ouse from St Ives to St Neots. Nottinghamshire prepares us for the north, and the building materials, of which it has its fair share, have a more sombre northern look about them. It is perhaps better equipped in this respect than Derbyshire, its western neighbour, but what the latter may lack in good stone, it more than makes up for in the most spectacular scenery of the region. Over towards Staffordshire, the great national park of the Peak affords endless enjoyment of nature's bounty. With so much, it might be unduly covetous to expect good churches as well. It has much of interest, but the attentions of the Victorians are all too evident. Derbyshire is, in fact, more a county for houses than for churches. The forest of great spires stretching from west Huntingdonshire right across to Derbyshire only starts to tail off as one approaches the north.

8 THE NORTHERN MARCHES AND YORKSHIRE

(CUMBERLAND, DURHAM, LANCASHIRE, NORTHUMBERLAND, WESTMORLAND AND YORKSHIRE)

Southerners tend to regard the cultural focus of the country as being in the south-east but this was far from the case in Anglo-Saxon times. In fact Sussex was one of the last counties to be evangelized. Until the frail organization of the Church was almost destroyed by the Viking invasions in the eighth century, civilization lay in Northumbria. The learned Bede, Alcuin and Aldhelm were the torch-bearers in that uncertain world.

The conversion of the north was initially in the hands of St Paulinus, an Italian monk, who joined St Augustine in Britain four years after the latter's arrival. Like Augustine, Paulinus found that the way was prepared for him by a woman. Ethelburga, a Kentish noblewoman, allowed him to accompany her when she travelled north to marry Edwin, King of Northumbria. Acceptance of the Christian faith was rapid, but unfortunately the Church collapsed when Edwin was killed in battle. It was left to Aidan, a monk from Iona, imbued with Celtic rather than Roman traditions, to make a second conversion, working from his monastery at Lindisfarne on Holy Island.

Anglo-Saxon. Benedict Biscop's churches at Monkwearmouth and Jarrow, and the contemporary church of Escomb have been mentioned in Chapter 1. Suffice it to state here that these are some of the earliest remains of Christian churches north of the Alps, and it was at Jarrow that the Venerable Bede spent nearly all his life.

The seventh and eighth centuries, before the Vikings started their harrying and pillaging, were periods of extraordinary artistic development, for which there was no parallel on the Continent. One has only to look at the Lindisfarne Gospels in the British Museum to understand what was achieved. Not surprisingly, in view of its origin, this great flowering of the spirit reflected Celtic culture. But this, in turn, was inspired by the east Mediterranean tradition of Egyptian monasticism, whence the Irish Church had been derived. Nowhere better can this be studied than in the standing crosses which have survived from those times. There are many of them, mostly in a fragmentary state, but one, at Bewcastle in Cumberland, is without question among the finest surviving pieces of early sculpture. It can be reliably dated as end of the seventh century and shows quite astonishing proficiency. The inspiration is Christian, for the figures of Christ and the two St Johns appear together with knots and vine scrolls. Bewcastle is not far from the Scottish border and for those prepared to go further north, there is an even finer cross at Ruthwell in Dumfriesshire.

The artistic mastery in this particular field was never achieved again in pre-Conquest times, although the building of crosses was resumed in the ninth and tenth centuries. One of the best examples is at Gosforth, also in Cumberland. The cross is very slender and the shaft, which is round at the base, becomes square higher up. It dates from the late tenth century; another, at Irton, is ninth century.

There are no pre-Conquest churches on the scale of Stow or Brixworth left in the region, but there are tantalizing remnants, of which perhaps the most evocative are the crypts of Hexham Priory church and of Ripon Cathedral. Hexham was founded by the fiery, arrogant Wilfrid, a man in the mould of Becket and Wolsey, who caused endless problems to his superiors, but who, at one time, was bishop of the whole of Northumbria. Later he became Bishop of Ripon (a see for five years in the seventh century) and Abbot of Hexham. From the writings of his biographer, Eddius, we know that in his time Hexham was a building of great importance, of *mirabili longitudine et altitudine*'. Wilfrid's chair also remains at Hexham. This tub-shaped stone seat with solid arms and back of equal height is a moving reminder of this great evangelist who was eventually sent to Sussex, the last stronghold of paganism in those days. Another similar seat, called a frith-stool, can be seen at Beverley Minster.

However, most of what is left from this period consists of towers, although Kirk Hammerton in the West Riding of Yorkshire is a complete church even if incorporated into a Victorian building, and Corbridge, one of the early Northumbrian churches, has both tower (pl. 68) and chancel dating from this period. The tower includes both early and late

Saxon features. Among the other towers are Bywell and Ovingham in Northumberland, Billingham and Norton in County Durham, Appleton-le-Street and Hovingham in the North Riding and Skipwith (except the top stage) and Wharram-le-Street in the East Riding. They are mainly western, but Norton has a rare crossing tower.

In the North Riding church of Brompton-in-Allertonshire is a quite irresistible set of Anglo-Danish hogback tombstones, with the charming addition of bears at each end sitting up and facing one another.

Norman. The north was a turbulent part of the country in mediaeval times. First, William had to subdue the north and this he did in a campaign of unequalled savagery. During the harrying of the north in 1069, not a house was left standing between Durham and York and no human beings left alive that could be smoked out. To quote G. M. Trevelyan, 'most of the North Riding and much of the East Riding of Yorkshire were depopulated by massacre' and 'many scores of villages were still without inhabitants seventeen years later'.

The mark of the Conqueror is nowhere expressed more forcibly than in the cathedral of Durham, built in a very short period of time to remind the northern people that no local independence would be permitted. The prince-bishop of the County Palatine of Durham was given secular and spiritual control over the whole region and it is not altogether surprising, therefore, to learn that the cathedral is generally regarded as the finest piece of Romanesque architecture in Europe, let alone England. The view of the cathedral and the great castle adjoining it from the other side of the River Wear is one of the greatest architectural thrills in the country.

This mighty building, with its massive, grooved piers, exerted considerable influence on architectural forms elsewhere, for example, the appearance of the spiral grooves at Waltham Abbey, Essex. They also occur at Selby and in the crypt at York Minster, at Kirkby Lonsdale in Westmorland and six miles away from Durham at Pittington, but here the grooves are in relief and not incised.

The Normans revived the monastery of Lindisfarne and, at Tynemouth, founded another. Both were Benedictine houses and were initially placed under Durham. Today only ruins remain of these once extensive buildings. In Northumberland, one of the best parish churches dating from this time is Norham, although it has suffered much from Victorian restoration. The village belonged to the bishops of Durham, who had a castle there, and the influence of Durham is reflected in the church. Other Norman churches in the county are Bolam and, among smaller ones, Seaton Delaval and isolated Thockrington, both of which have richly ornamented arches.

Yorkshire has much Norman work of all kinds and, among decorative work, can show noteworthy examples of fonts, arches, capitals and doorways, the 'most distinguishing marks of Norman architecture' in profusion. The village churches of Adel near Leeds, Birkin (pl. 64) and Healaugh are especially enjoyable. Weaverthorpe, in the North Riding, has a typical example of a plain, unbuttressed tower with bell-openings in the top displaced to one side for a stair-turret.

Even among these riches the crypt of Lastingham in the North Riding is outstanding. An early Norman construction, it forms part of the monastery refounded on the beautiful site where St Chad's brother, St Cedd, set up the original monastery in 654. Of late work, the south doorway at Fishlake in the West Riding is possibly the most sumptuously decorated in Yorkshire. Near the border of the East Riding, Farnham has a beautiful chancel, the remnant of a Norman church.

St Bees in Cumberland has a fine Norman doorway which dates from about 1160. It is richly decorated and is of three orders. The rest of the church shows good Norman work. Isel, (pl. 60) is a small country church of *c.* 1130.

Lancashire, in common with its mediaeval representation generally, is weak in Norman work and apart from the major monastic houses of Furness Abbey and Cartmel Priory there is little of note to record.

Among furnishings, and this almost invariably means stone in Norman times, there is a wealth of elaborately carved fonts. One of the best is the rectangular example at Bridekirk in Cumberland (the rest of the church is Victorian). Other good examples are those at Bowness-on-Solway, also in Cumberland, North Grimston, Kirkburn, Cowlam and Langtoft in the East Riding and Thorpe Salvin in the West Riding.

At Church Kelloe, not far from Durham, is a rare piece of sculpture probably dating from the twelfth century. In the shape of a cross, it shows three scenes connected with the finding of the Holy Cross by the Empress Helena.

Bronze door-knockers are always a joy. How thankfully a man on the run must have grasped them when they acted as symbols of sanctuary in more troubled times. There are fine ones at Warboys in Huntingdon-shire and Dormington in Herefordshire, but the most famous of all is the one on the north entrance door at Durham Cathedral. At Adel is one of fine quality and great appeal depicting a monster devouring a man whose forlorn head appears out of its mouth. This church and Durham Cathedral set the seal on the perfect contrast in Norman building of an exquisite small village church and a mighty cathedral. There must be few counties in England, apart from Herefordshire, which provide so much of outstanding interest from the twelfth century as Yorkshire and Durham.

Early English. After the harrying of the north, there was a period of calm until Edward I marched into Scotland and carried off the corona-tion stone of Scone to England. Prior to that, the north of England and mediaeval Scotland had enjoyed a golden age. During this period, the Cistercians established themselves in Yorkshire and accumulated great wealth from the rearing of sheep. They led, however, a solitary life and the influence of their austere style of building was not felt until later.

The rebuilding of the choir at Canterbury was a more powerful force in the evolution of Gothic in England, although, as mentioned in Chapter 1, the exact course of events is not yet fully understood. The style may well have come from the Middle East, where shortage of timber meant that great beams could not be laid across wide spans, thus making some form of stone vaulting necessary. From the Middle East the style was brought back to the great Burgundian monastic houses.

The transition from Norman to Early English in the north is not always easy to follow and, in some parts, especially in the north-western counties of Cumberland, Westmorland and Lancashire, very little of this style survives. Fine fonts remain at Aspatria and Cross Canonby, but the highlight is the west front of Lanercost Priory (pl. 70) (now a parish church) which contains in the gable a very rare thirteenth-century statue of St Mary Magdalene.

Lancashire's sole contribution comes from a former priory. Cartmel (pl. 74), with its unique tower (the top square stage is set diagonally on the lower portion), was begun about 1190 as a priory for Augustinian Canons, although most of the building is later.

The north-eastern counties show a different picture. In Northumberland, the late twelfth and early thirteenth century was a peak of building activity. Brinkburn, Tynemouth and Hexham all show signs of vigorous and effective Early English work. Tynemouth is a ruin and so was Brinkburn until restored in the nineteenth century, but Hexham has been in continuous use. The distinguishing marks of northern thirteenth-century work are long, tall and narrow chancels and elongated lancets. Examples of Northumberland chancels are too numerous to list, but the style can nowhere be better seen than at Haltwhistle. This is a complete Early English church, punctuated throughout with narrow lancets (pl. 69). Other Northumbrian features are tall, blank arcades on shafts round the chancel as at Bamburgh, and the low tunnel-vault to be seen at Kirknewton. Despite its lack of height, there is something very spirited and forceful about this vault.

There is much to see in County Durham. Of more usual features, the chancels at Darlington, the naves there and at Hartlepool and, among country places, Sedgefield, where there are stiff-leaf capitals, are outstanding. Of less common features, the thirteenth-century broach spire at West Boldon is especially striking in a county that can boast only five mediaeval stone spires. Hartlepool and Darlington both have thirteenth-century towers. The finest show of lancets is at Houghton-le-Spring, which has a row of eight in the chancel south wall.

Yorkshire is a county of contrasts and this is very apparent in its parish churches. The East Riding is one of the areas in England where building on a grand scale prevailed, and the thirteenth century ushered in an era of the most magnificent architecture, of which Pevsner regards the period 1250–1350 as the climax. In the West Riding, on the west front of Ripon Cathedral, is one of the most splendid grouping of lancets in the whole country.

The staircase leading to the reading desk in the refectory of Beaulieu Abbey in Hampshire was mentioned in Chapter 5. Beverley Minster has a double one leading from the north choir aisle to the former chapter house. It is hard to choose between these gems of Early English work of the 1230s.

There are smaller churches, too, and perhaps none more appealing than Filey in the popular seaside resort at the north-east tip of the East Riding. A complete building of this style, it is nevertheless Yorkshire in the rugged simplicity of its short crossing tower and the sturdy stone of which it is built. At Hessle in the same Riding is a hint of what mediaeval churches might have looked like when they were painted, for here the scrolls on the capitals still retain some of their colour. This is most unusual, for these areas have normally long since lost any trace of the original colouring.

The construction of Skelton, four miles north-west of York, was undoubtedly influenced by the masons of that city, for there is competent stiff-leaf and a high degree of grace and refinement. Nun Monkton in the West Riding was founded about 1150 as a Benedictine nunnery. Its nave and west front together form an interesting example of the transition from Norman to Gothic. The church is most delightfully situated at the end of the village green, next to the Hall.

In this northern area the Cistercians left some of the most substantial and romantic ruins to be seen anywhere and, although technically outside the scope of this book, mention must be made of Fountains, Rievaulx and Bolton in Yorkshire, and Furness in Lancashire, for here the Early English style is at its purest and clearest.

Decorated. The lack of security in this region during the Middle Ages was at no time felt more acutely than during the Decorated period. This uncertainty and the constant raiding by the Scots is reflected in the dearth of good church architecture. The masons were more concerned with building castles than churches. In the region of Cumberland and Westmorland there is only Appleby in the latter, but otherwise the mood of the times is best reflected in fortified towers, such as those at Newton Arlosh, Great Salkeld and Burgh-by-Sands. The flowing tracery of the fourteenth century, which is so much in evidence elsewhere, is not found in the north.

It is the same in Durham and Lancashire. There is no early or mid-fourteenth-century church in the whole of Durham, and Lancashire's contribution is confined to the south chapel of Cartmel. The lack of abbeys and priories in south Lancashire is perhaps also symptomatic of the general uncertainty of the time.

Yorkshire shows signs of more building activity in this period, and a local characteristic is the straight-headed window with ogee tracery, for example Skipwith, but even as far south as the North and West Ridings we have to search hard. The beautiful ruins of Guisborough Priory show the form of tracery in that century and the choir of Selby is a notable example of the Decorated style. A rarity is the bridge chapel. Of only four remaining in the country, there are two in Yorkshire, at Wakefield and Rotherham and the other two are at St Ives, Huntingdonshire and Bradford-on-Avon, Wiltshire. But Wakefield is by far the finest, although heavily restored and in parts rebuilt. The Decorated chancel at Fishlake contrasts with the south doorway already mentioned. Perhaps the most moving memorial of the era is the village church of Thornton-le-Dale in the North Riding set most happily at the end of an attractive village.

It is only in the East Riding that the cloud of mediaeval warfare lifted and there is evidence of a more settled life. The cloth trade and sheep-rearing brought great prosperity to this area, and many signs can be seen of the wealth that existed in the fourteenth century. Foremost among these are the church of Patrington, then the north chapel of St Mary, Beverley, the initial work at Holy Trinity, Kingston-upon-Hull, and a fine group of stone screens.

Patrington must rate as one of the finest Decorated churches in England, set off in a marvellous way with its superb spire. The space between the square tower and the octagonal spire is bridged by an octagonal openwork screen, a unique and very successful experiment. The interior is of noble proportions and the nave capitals are some of the most beautiful stone carving to be seen anywhere.

Decorated work at its most ornate can be seen upon the Percy tomb at Beverley Minster, one of the most elaborate examples of fully fledged fourteenth-century ornamentation in the country.

Towers. The comparative barrenness of the land during the Middle Ages in the far north did not breed fine towers. There is a general squareness about the churches which is accentuated by short, low towers, for example, Great Salkeld, Skipton and Dent, but they are appropriate, as so often with English mediaeval building, to their surroundings. Yorkshire is different. There was not only wealth in the East Riding but the resources that went with it. Spires are not frequent but, apart from Patrington, there is the truly prodigious spire of Hemingbrough (pl. 63), representing nearly two-thirds of the combined height of tower and spire, all wrong by the text-book but a success none the less.

According to some architectural experts, towers should taper towards the top in order to correct the perspective of the eye. In the north, on the contrary, the top stage is often corbelled out, as at Beetham, West-morland (pl. 72), and Staindrop, Durham (pl. 67). There is a group around Leeds, of which Batley, Ledsham and Whitkirk are representa-tive, where the parapets are thus handled. At Whitkirk the parapets of the whole church are treated in this way. Once again, local individuality succeeds despite the experts, and provides further regional variety for the questing church lover. There are eleven stone spires in the East Riding, (of which Ottringham and Wintringham are two further examples), thirteen in the West, but only a few in the North.

Perpendicular towers. Professor Allen divides the many notable towers of the East and West Ridings into those which show a Somerset influence and those which do not. The reason for this influence is interesting. Two of the bishops of Bath and Wells went north towards the end of the fourteenth century just when towers were being built without spires and they took with them the ideas that were crystallizing in the south. One of the bishops even gave to Skirlaugh, his native village, a fine church which included a much-pinnacled small tower. Two of the finest of the Somerset-influenced towers are at Great Driffield, which shows commendable restraint and attention to detail, and Tick-hill, just over the border from Nottinghamshire. Others are at Hatfield and Pocklington.

Tickhill is a very early Perpendicular tower, and also shows the Yorkshire influence in the use of the local fashion of cresting or triangular decoration above the embrasures of the battlements. Another Yorkshire trait is the employment of very lofty and almost disproportionately large belfry windows, which Howden has in very pronounced form. The purely Yorkshire towers also include Holy Trinity, Hull, the twin west towers of Beverley Minster, the south-west tower of Bridlington, the crossing tower of St Mary's, Beverley, and Hedon, the best of all. All have pinnacles at the corners as well as intermediate ones, and some, such as Skirlaugh and Holme-upon-Spalding-Moor, also have them on the buttresses. Ecclesfield in the West Riding is another fine tower.

Two towers, Sancton in the East Riding and Coxwold in the North, are octagonal from the ground up, and some authorities regard Sancton as the best of all octagonal towers. Pontefract and Laughton-en-le-Morthen are among the towers in the West Riding which have an octagonal top stage.

Timber towers of the Essex type are represented by a solitary example at Raskelf in the North Riding.

Perpendicular. The main centre of building activity was again in the East Riding. Here, the Perpendicular style is seen at its best in the six grand church towers of St Mary's, Beverley; Beverley Minster; Holy Trinity, Hull; Bridlington; Hedon and Howden. The west front of the Minster, with its twin towers, is surely one of the most impressive in all England. Holy Trinity, Hull, is the largest parish church in the country; it has an extremely long interior and the slim pillars of the nave are typical of early Perpendicular building. Bridlington was at one time an important priory of the Augustinian Canons and measured over three hundred feet in length. But, as at Snettisham (Norfolk), the Dissolution robbed it of its choir. More of a piece is St Mary's, Beverley. This, too, has a splendid nave, and is regarded by many people as one of the most beautiful churches in England. How is it that a town the size of Beverley has two churches of the scale and magnificence of the Minster and St Mary's? The only possible suggestion is that the Minster was a college for secular priests, while St Mary's was the parish church.

Another feature of this favoured part of England is the stone screens which are probably finer and more numerous than in any other county, for instance, the pulpitum at Howden, which is now used as a reredos. Nor can one omit the bench-ends at Hemingbrough. At St Mary's, Beverley, is the popular favourite of the Maynstrells (minstrels). These are set round one of the piers, 'a famous, funny and lovable group', as Pevsner describes them. This group of strolling entertainers helped to finance the building of the nave piers. Others concerned in raising money for the building were John Crossley and his wife, and the Wyffes (wives) of Beverley – an early example of the great help which churches receive from the ladies of the parish.

Elsewhere, Yorkshire is not so rich in architecture of this period. The West Riding participated in the prosperity of the fifteenth and early sixteenth centuries as the churches at Rotherham, Wakefield (now a cathedral) and Halifax show. Those Victorian architects, the Scotts, have made their hand felt at the first two, and the mediaeval atmosphere has been impaired as a result of this and the rash of industrial growth which surrounds them. Nevertheless, Rotherham is still the focal point of what is now a large town, and nothing can obscure the 250 feet of

Wakefield's spire. For something less urban, Ecclesfield is a fairly complete Perpendicular church with battlements. In the North Riding, the main fifteenth-century church is Thirsk, admirably grouped with a fine Georgian hall. Others are Askrigg, Coxwold which has a rather tweedy texture, and Bedale, which watches so effectively over the little town below it.

These two ridings are not very flush with furnishings, although there are a few fine items. The font-covers at Almondbury and Selby, for example, are elaborate yet delicate; and the late fifteenth-century wall-paintings at Pickering are one of the most complete sets, if not the most artistic, in the country. A unique item is the fifteenth-century cross-head at Sherburn-in-Elmet; the Crucifixion is carved on both sides and is pierced right through with tracery and the whole is surmounted with a gable. Finally, the wooden screen at Aysgarth still retains its ribbed coving, and the fourteenth-century chest at Wath is one of the most richly decorated in England.

In the East Riding, the misericords at Beverley Minster are unrivalled for their number and quality. In the same area, the rood-screen at Flamborough is one of the very few to retain its loft (most of the others are in Wales).

County Durham has some notable east windows, of which Brancepeth and Norton are two examples; and a few fine porches, Staindrop (pl. 67) being one. Boltongate in Cumberland has a particularly interesting Perpendicular church and there is a fine west porch at Abbey Town (previously Holme Cultram Monastery). In Westmorland, Kendal and Appleby experienced a touch of wool wealth, which is reflected in the addition of aisles. This is also seen at Kirkby Lonsdale.

Stone. Durham Cathedral was built of a good carboniferous sandstone and today the same millstone grit is used when repairs are necessary. Northumberland, Durham, south Yorkshire and Lancashire are well supplied with this stone, although it varies in quality and some is too rough for building purposes. In Durham there are also limestones in the west of the county and, in the east, near South Shields, is the thin strip of magnesian limestone which has continued northwards from Nottinghamshire. Granitic rocks help to form the Cheviots, but the main material in Northumberland is sandstone. This can be of the millstone grit type or of other formations, and it might be true to say that Northumberland has more sandstone buildings than any other county, although the next region – the west Midlands – is certainly the sandstone region *par excellence.*

Lancashire has a complex geological pattern, but the net result is not very encouraging to the builder. It is, as Alec Clifton-Taylor has pointed out, a county very largely of brick, sometimes of a 'screaming red'. There is, none the less, plenty of sandstone – again of variable quality. New red sandstone is being used in the new Liverpool Anglican cathedral but, further north, there are carboniferous sandstones which stand up well to the industrial atmosphere of those parts. Beyond the Ribble there is limestone of a light grey colour, also from the Carboniferous system. This tends to be rather rubbly, which applies even more to the older Silurian stone used at Hawkshead church (pl. 73).

In the Lake District there is a great spectrum of stones, some of volcanic origin. Perhaps nowhere else in the area is there such a range of colours, some due to staining by oxides, others to the stone itself. In general, the northern part of Cumberland and south-east along the coast from St Bees is pink or brown, due to the presence of new red sandstones and also, in the south, to granites. Westmorland is, on the other hand, mainly a grey county, obtaining its stone from Silurian and even Ordovician formations, but including a carboniferous lime-stone to the north-east and south-east of the county.

As can be seen, there was no lack of stone, but oolite was not one of those available, except in very small quantities from Brough to the north of York in the East Riding. The region was, in fact, self-sufficient, for in Yorkshire, apart from the magnesian limestone, there were other limestones and many sandstones which suited all needs. Where there was a deficiency, as in the East Riding, stone was brought from the West Riding. Millstone grit has played a big part and, although its rough, pebbly texture does not make it a very gracious stone, it is eminently suited for the conditions where it is found. The rugged Pennine country and the industrial areas situated on the coal measures do not suit the more urbane limestones found further south. The grit of the north can accept some grit in the stone.

General. The picture is of an impoverishment in the far north which gradually gives way to easier conditions as one travels south and culminates in the quite exceptional wealth of the East Riding. Apart from Yorkshire, only in County Durham does one escape to some extent the effects of constant warring, possibly because, under its prince-bishops, it was better able to defend itself. Lancashire also suffered from the general poverty, for the coal measures which brought industrial wealth in the nineteenth century only supported bleak moorlands in the Middle Ages.

Nevertheless, if one is prepared to accept these limitations, there is much to enjoy – the small, the humble and rough-textured, for example, Isel (pl. 60) in Cumberland and Grasmere (pl. 71) in Westmorland, and Hubberholme in the West Riding, which still retains its rood-loft dating from 1558. They all have their own especial charm and they accord perfectly with the local environment. So often, too, the enjoyment of a church is enhanced by the beauty of its setting, choosing examples is invidious, but Nun Monkton in the West Riding, Thornton-le-Dale and West Tanfield (pl. 65) in the North Riding, and Grinton, in Swaledale, are particularly fine.

Nowhere can one feel more keenly the strength of monastic foundations and the great part they played in mediaeval life, the beautiful remote sites they chose even today bring calm and tranquillity to the traveller. Yorkshire must be supreme for romantic ruins and it may be that the skills the monks fostered in raising sheep helped to bring the extraordinary yield in wealth and buildings of the East Riding.

In general, the splendour of the churches is in inverse ratio to the magnificence of the scenery and if, in some of the poorer parts, there are fewer remains than elsewhere, in compensation there are some of the grandest landscapes that the country possesses.

9 WEST MIDLANDS

(CHESHIRE, HEREFORDSHIRE, SHROPSHIRE, STAFFORDSHIRE, WARWICKSHIRE
AND WORCESTERSHIRE)

This area was, in the main, converted to Christianity by the followers
of St Aidan, who travelled down the west side of the country from
Northumbria. It is significant, too, that the most important cathedral
of the region, Lichfield, was dedicated to St Chad, the Celtic missionary.
For sixteen years, in the heyday of Mercia's power, it was even the seat
of an archbishop.

Much of the west Midlands area borders on Wales and, in some
parts of Herefordshire and Shropshire, the Saxons never fully subdued
the previous British occupiers. When Offa, the great King of Mercia,
built his famous dyke from the River Wye to the River Dee, he set a
limit on further expansion westwards, while at the same time creating
a bulwark against Welsh infiltration.

Towards the end of the Saxon era, Staffordshire and Cheshire suffered devastation at the hands of Edmund Ironside for refusing to support him against Canute, his rival to the throne. After the Norman
Conquest, Staffordshire suffered at the hands of William I when he
suppressed a local rebellion in 1069.

The subsequent history of the region was one of the gradual dis-
possession of the Welsh as the Lords Marcher carved out for themselves
semi-independent feudal estates. There were, however, brief periods
of national revival when the spirit of nationalism roused the Welsh
people to fight for independence. The first major rebellion led by Llewelyn
ap Griffith, was crushed at the end of the thirteenth century by Edward I,
who, to assert his authority, built a string of castles across the Princi-
pality and created his infant son, Edward, Prince of Wales.

A more serious attempt was made by the great patriot, Owen Glen-
dower, at the beginning of the fifteenth century. An English force was

defeated in battle and Owen marched into England, setting fire to the city of Worcester.

Despite these alarums and excursions, however, the counties bordering on Wales did not suffer to anything like the same extent as those bordering on Scotland and architecture had a better chance to establish itself.

Anglo-Saxon. Possibly because of incomplete conquest by the Anglo-Saxons, there is no other region with so little pre-Conquest architecture, or even sculpture, as this one. It is, in this respect, in complete contrast with the east Midlands. A ninth-century cross-head at Cropthorne in Worcestershire, the Sandbach crosses in Cheshire and the lower part of the tower of Wootton Wawen in Warwickshire are virtually the only notable remains. There are, nevertheless, no fewer than four Saxon arches in the tower of Wootton Wawen and the entire ground-floor area is eleventh century, blocking off the nave from the chancel behind. It is a striking example of what a church of that date might have looked like.

The gospels of St Chad at Lichfield Cathedral are particularly fine. Dating from the early eighth century, these manuscripts are of Lindisfarne quality and may well be based on Lindisfarne work. They include the complete gospels according to St Matthew and St Mark together with three chapters of the Gospel of St Luke. They are of the utmost value in showing the degree of artistic mastery achieved.

Norman. If the Anglo-Saxon architectural yield is poor, the Norman is rich beyond compare. Herefordshire is one of the most exciting Norman counties in the kingdom, with its quite distinctive local school of decoration, combining Celtic, Scandinavian, French and even Italian influences. Kilpeck (pl. 81) is one of the most elaborately carved Norman village churches in the country. Fortunately, the work was carried out in a sandstone which was more resistant than most, and it remains crisp and alive today. Moccas, built of tufa with sandstone doorways, is another complete Norman village church but without such elaborate carving. Norman sculpture can be seen at its most exuberant in the fonts of Castle Frome and Eardisley, and in the tympana of Brinsop, Stratton Sugwas and Fownhope, where it is now inside the church. The influence is also felt in Worcestershire in the font of Chaddesley Corbett. In Shropshire, the outstanding piece of Norman sculpture is the tympanum of Aston Eyre, near Much Wenlock, showing the Palm Sunday entry into Jerusalem; Much Wenlock Priory itself, although now a ruin, also has two pieces of the highest interest.

The west portal of the priory church of Leominster (pl. 80) has spirited capitals showing two birds, two reapers and two writhing serpents.

In Worcestershire, many of the twelfth-century buildings are notable for their size and there are nearly thirty which have naves or chancels from this period, for example, Astley and Broadway. This county is even stronger than Herefordshire in monastic remains used as parish churches. Evesham, Pershore and Malvern make an impressive trio – Malvern with a nave of the grandeur of Malmesbury, and Pershore with crossing, transepts and the stump of a nave from this period. Sometimes the choir had to be sacrificed at the Dissolution, in other cases, the nave. At Pershore, the parts remaining, which include also the later chancel and tower, would have disappeared too, if the parishioners had not clubbed together to save them. At Evesham, apart from the famous tower, only the entrance arch to the chapter house and portions of two gateways remain but, within the abbey precincts, there is the well-known feature, still not fully explained, of two churches within one churchyard, one of which, All Saints, has a mainly Norman interior. Worcester Cathedral was a monastic foundation, belonging to the Benedictines.

A local trait is the projection of doorways from the wall with blind arcading above. Eastham church in Worcestershire (pl. 83) is a good example of this. This little church is largely built of tufa (see Chapter 2), a material also used at Shelsley Walsh and Hanley William in the same county.

Shropshire, too, has much to offer. The conquerors made a semi-independent unit of the county and the Norman lord founded the Benedictine abbey of St Mary, Shrewsbury, which still retains the feeling of forcefulness so characteristic of early Norman architecture. The same lord also founded the Cluniac priory of Much Wenlock, the sculpture of which was mentioned above. The west front of Much Wenlock church is a telling example of early Norman work. Later Norman building can be seen in a large number of churches, but there are two well above average – the little chapel of Heath, standing alone in the fields and consisting only of nave and chancel without even a bellcote, and the village church of Linley. Heath is one of those endearing examples of twelfth-century country places of worship such as Steetley in Derbyshire, Tickencote and Tixover in Rutland, Adel in Yorkshire and in which the south-east is so particularly rich. The font of Stottesdon (of almost Herefordshire calibre), the doorway at Edstaston and the chancel arch of Stirchley are outstanding.

Compared with this, and apart from the cathedral, Cheshire can only muster the nave of St John's church in Chester and a doorway at Norton. This scarcity may be due to the lack of monastic foundations, because the only major religious house at that time was Benedictine Chester.

Staffordshire has a notable Norman church at Tutbury, well sited near the castle and overlooking the town. The sumptuous west front includes a doorway of seven orders which is one of the finest in England. The somewhat heavy nave is early work of about 1100. St Mary, Stafford, has a remarkable font and the chancel arch is also Norman. Pattingham, in the same county, has a Norman north arcade.

Warwickshire is fairly well endowed with work of this period. The main attraction is Berkswell, near Coventry, which has a rib-vaulted crypt and is the outstanding twelfth-century church of the county. The nave is wide, as is also the nave at Stoneleigh. Other churches of the period are the early one at Ryton-on-Dunsmore and Wyken.

Early English. After all this building activity in Herefordshire, Worcestershire and Shropshire, there came a lull, perhaps because needs were satisfied. None of these counties are rich in Early English work, nor, for that matter, are Warwickshire and Cheshire. Nevertheless, the style made its impact, especially at the larger churches. Of these, Abbey Dore in Herefordshire is one of the most interesting. A retrochoir and double ambulatory were added to a short chancel which still retains Norman capitals although building did not start before 1175–80. The richly shafted piers and the noble ambulatory make a striking demonstration of how the early severity of the Cistercian style softened later into something more human and, although the nave has disappeared and a seventeenth-century tower been added, this remnant of an important Cistercian abbey is superb Early English. Apart from this, the best thirteenth-century work in Herefordshire is the Lady Chapel of the cathedral.

Merevale, Warwickshire, was a smaller Cistercian abbey but only fragments remain. The parish church has only two bays in the short but wide Early English nave, this contrasts with a Perpendicular chancel of four bays, so producing a curiously unbalanced effect. The west front and chancel arch are also thirteenth century. Northfield and Pillerton Hersey have fine chancels in this style, the latter with a priest's doorway.

As in Herefordshire, a monastic foundation is the main Early English feature in Shropshire. This is the remnant of the ruined Much Wenlock Priory church, but it was never a parish church so, according to the terms of this book, St Mary, Shrewsbury, is the county's best example of this style of architecture. St Mary's has an exceptionally fine nave arcade built about the turn of the twelfth/thirteenth centuries with beautiful stiff-leaf capitals. The building as a whole is a notable example of the slow-growth mediaeval parish church, showing all styles, which is typical of the Midlands. At Acton Burnell is an Early English font of exceptional quality.

The most notable thirteenth-century work in Worcestershire is in the church of St Andrew, Droitwich, and in a number of chancels, particularly Kempsey, Overbury and Ripple. The south chapel at Bredon is also worthy of mention.

Cheshire is thin in Early English work and, once more, the best is at St John, Chester, where the clerestory is Early English. Apart from that, Acton, near Nantwich, is the only early nave arcade and Prestbury the only late one; while Rushton, isolated on a ridge, has its original timber nave.

Staffordshire has rather more Early English remains. There is, in fact, much to see from the period and some is of outstanding merit. Checkley in the north, and Clifton Campville (pronounced without the 'p') in the south, are mediaeval churches of great character with fine, lofty interiors. The nave and clerestory of Checkley and the north transept of Clifton are thirteenth century. There are also chancels of this period at Alrewas and Brewood, while Coppenhall has an authentic village church of about 1220. Gnosall, a collegiate church, is largely thirteenth century and Bradley has a nave arcade of *c*. 1260.

Decorated. Building activity during this period was uneven. Whereas in Herefordshire there was a recession of building after the turn of the twelfth century, the Decorated period in Warwickshire was a busy one and there is plenty to see in a composed and undramatic mood. Staffordshire has Checkley and Clifton Campville, already referred to, and Cheshire begins to make its presence felt with its town churches of Nantwich and Stockport and the smaller church of Astbury. In Shropshire, the fourteenth century tends to merge into Perpendicular in a way which makes exact division difficult. For instance, at Battlefield, built by Henry IV in expiation for the heavy casualties suffered at the Battle of Shrewsbury, there are fourteenth- and fifteenth-century windows alongside one another. Most of the Decorated work is in window tracery and especially in the magnificent east window of St Mary's, Shrewsbury, with its Jesse tree in contemporary stained glass. Stottesdon has much fourteenth-century work, but the emphasis in this county is more on the Perpendicular than the Decorated period.

In Warwickshire, Coleshill is another mixture of fourteenth- and fifteenth-century styles, part of the nave arcades being of the former and part of the latter. So, too, is Solihull, where the chancel, crossing and sumptuous north chapel are all of Decorated work. Aston Cantlow has a fine chancel and there is fourteenth-century work in smaller churches such as Grendon and Harborough Magna. Astley and Tanworth-in-Arden are more obviously Decorated, but, perhaps more enjoyable than either, is the little church of St Peter ad Vincula, at Ratley in the south-eastern part of the county. In this small building one can experience the full impact of the style, for there were few later additions. The piers are without capitals so that they sweep into the arches. Brailes (pl. 87) which was under the advowson of Kenilworth Priory, is another example of the Decorated style.

The show-pieces of Herefordshire are the chancel of Madley, built on generous and spacious lines, and the north chapel of Ledbury. Madley's outstandingly fine tower will be dealt with later. Of interest here is the polygonal apse. Although a rare feature (see also Bluntisham in Huntingdonshire) there is another in Herefordshire, at Marden. The Ledbury chapel is believed to have been built by the same masons who worked with such skill at Leominster. At both churches, great play is made of the favourite ball-flower ornament.

Strangely enough, ball-flower decoration does not occur at all in Cheshire, but this does not detract from the impact made by Nantwich. Here is a fine church, which draws all eyes to its striking octagonal tower. Inside is a handsome chancel with a fine timber roof and many bosses. Below, the twenty fourteenth-century stalls, with their elaborate canopies, are the best in the area. The hilarious set of misericords includes a woman beating her husband with a ladle (reminiscent of the sgraffito at Leighton Linslade church in Bedfordshire), the devil pulling a man's mouth open and a fox pretending to be dead.

Northwich, another of the salt or 'wich' towns, has a stone reredos, not perhaps in the Christchurch, Hampshire, category, but rare because it is original.

The highlight of Worcestershire is the crossing tower of Pershore, otherwise Hadzor, Sedgeberrow, both heavily restored, and Dodderhill are mainly Decorated, and Chaddesley Corbett, mentioned before in connection with its Norman font, has a charming chancel. Broadway possesses a delightful south chapel.

As in the case of Early English, Staffordshire might claim to hold the palm for Decorated work. There are two outstanding churches: Checkley, which has a glorious chancel with good sixteenth-century stalls and much old glass, and Clifton Campville (pl. 88), with its noble spire and spacious interior with good roof. Apart from these there are a whole range of interesting churches: isolated Rolleston, Wychford and Sandon all mostly of the fourteenth century; Norbury with nave and chancel of about 1340 together with original roof; among partly Decorated churches, Alstonfield, Mayfield with a fourteenth-century chancel, topped by a scalloped parapet; and two town churches, Tamworth and St Mary, Stafford, with its Early English north transept.

Perpendicular. This is not a wool region but, on the other hand, it contains some rich arable land and fine pasture, not to mention the Cheshire salt industry, all of which helped to produce a good average level of income in the Middle Ages. These were not the conditions, however, to make for spectacular Perpendicular architecture, which, to a large extent, depended upon large individual fortunes. Pevsner writes that 'there are no Perpendicular buildings of the first order in Herefordshire'. Warwickshire was more prosperous than the rest and St Mary, Warwick, and Holy Trinity, Coventry, are in the grand class. This, of course, leaves out St Michael's which, because of its fate in the war, has given way as cathedral to Sir Basil Spence's much discussed new building. The Beauchamp Chapel, in St Mary, Warwick, with its almost regal monument to the Earl of Warwick, whose effigy is cast in bronze, is one of the most sumptuous constructions of its date in the whole of England. Other churches are Knowle, St John, Coventry, Coughton and Weston-on-Avon, quite apart from the superb chancel of Stratford-on-Avon. The style continued into the reign of Edward VI, when the chancel aisles of Sutton Coldfield were built.

Shropshire shared in the general prosperity, but this is not reflected to the same extent in its parish churches. Probably Tong is the most famous, although rather cluttered with memorials to the Vernon family. The church was built after a chantry college was founded there in 1410. The other main items in the county are towers.

Towers are Worcestershire's chief contribution, but there are the churches of Claines and St Lawrence, Evesham, which are mainly Perpendicular and so, too, are the exterior and chancel of Great Malvern.

Cheshire can offer a whole range of fifteenth-century work at a number of large churches and some excellent woodwork in roofs and screens. There is only space to mention a few, but it is interesting to note the size of these churches, which are situated in relatively small towns but cover wide parishes. The best are Astbury (pl. 75), built of a good stratum of millstone grit, grey outside and pinkish inside, Malpas, on the Flintshire border, Great Budworth and Barthomley. Astbury can also claim pre-eminence in roof and screen, of which Mobberley, too, has fine examples. For situation, Gawsworth is particularly charming. The grouping of church, houses and water must be one of the best in the whole county and is worth visiting for that alone. However, the group of castle and church at Stokesay (pl. 78) in Shropshire is also hard to beat.

The town churches of Staffordshire – St Mary, Stafford, St Peter, Wolverhampton and the collegiate church of St Editha, Tamworth – are the most prominent of the late mediaeval period. Tamworth and Wolverhampton are both built on hills, as churches should be in towns. Tamworth has a stone screen at the west end which rises to the full height of the nave with striking effect. The stone pulpit at Wolverhampton is unique in retaining its original stone staircase. These are all worthy representatives of urban centres. Outstanding otherwise are the late fifteenth-century nave of Eccleshall, the sixteenth-century exterior of Penkridge and the earlier example at Alrewas. Some of these buildings have noteworthy towers.

Spires and towers. This is not an area where fine towers are very common. Nor is it mediaeval stone spire country, and yet it is estimated that, in Warwickshire, there are more than two dozen spires and that Worcestershire has almost as many but not all as tall. Staffordshire has quite a number, but many have been restored or rebuilt at a later date. Herefordshire has seven. They tail off in the north-west, Cheshire having five and Shropshire only three.

The influence of Somerset and Gloucestershire on towers is felt in Warwickshire and Worcestershire. The central tower of Great Malvern, built of sandstone and not of oolite, is modelled upon the parent tower of Gloucester Cathedral, but has one stage less and is more restrained in its panelled decoration. The superb free-standing tower of Evesham Abbey church, which, built in 1513 is late for this style, is completely covered with panelling on both outer and inner sides.

The towers of this region, however, are highly individual and are not easy to fit into categories. St Peter's, Wolverhampton, is a case in point, with its rich detail but formal outline without projections at the corners. Ludlow is remarkable for its height and satisfying outline, and makes a noble prospect from nearby Clee Hill.

Cheshire towers sometimes have a frieze below the battlements and many are well pinnacled.

Two octagonal towers, those at Nantwich, Cheshire, and Hodnett, Shropshire, call for special notice, because they are of this shape from the ground to the top. St Mary, Stafford, a central tower like Nantwich, is octagonal only in the upper stage.

Highly inventive are the towers of Brailes (pl. 87) in Warwickshire and of Gawsworth in Cheshire. In the latter, a rather bare middle stage is compensated by a fine top stage with eight pinnacles and eight gargoyles or grotesques below the parapet. It is a principle of good tower composition that the eye should be led towards the top and this is satisfied at Gawsworth.

If Herefordshire is not well endowed with towers, it can offer much that is peculiar to itself. The seven detached towers in the county are a local pleasure, especially the late fourteenth-century one at Pembridge. It is of three stages with a little spire on top, reminiscent of Essex. Those at Garway and Yarpole are thirteenth- and fourteenth-century respectively. Also of the thirteenth century is Bosbury, which, although in the east of the county, has fortified walls. A closer reminder of the proximity of Wales is the tower of Ewyas Harold which has walls over seven feet thick.

Pembridge and Yarpole have massive timber framing within. Timber plays an even bigger role in the more northern parts. Worcestershire has five timber towers, including Pirton and Warndon, and again one is reminded of the Essex towers.

An oddity in Warwickshire is the bell-turret at Baginton. This is polygonal with a spirelet and rests over the junction between nave and chancel. The little tower at St Kenelm's, Romsley, in Worcestershire is regarded by Professor Allen as the smallest tower in England not to be called a turret. It is half within the west wall of the nave and supported externally with two buttresses which are linked together with an arch. It has a panelled parapet and is decorated with carvings of large animals. The church is mainly of red sandstone but the tower is grey, which makes a delightful climax to this attractive little building, so near the industrial spread of Birmingham.

A list of towers for the region might well include Leek in Staffordshire, Bromsgrove and Kidderminster in Worcestershire, Sandbach, Acton, Barthomley and Wybunbury in Cheshire, Bromyard and Much Marcle in Herefordshire, and Knowle in Warwickshire.

Of spires, Weobley in Herefordshire, which has the refinement of flying buttresses connecting the spire with the pinnacles, is the outstanding example, but there are many others. They are all recessed and of the parapet type, e.g. Ross, Stoke Edith, Llangarron. Coleshill and Tredington are notable in Warwickshire, but the former is much rebuilt, being of unreliable sandstone. Tredington, on the other hand, is built of the delightful light brown Hornton stone. A lofty church, it is set in a well-tended churchyard and forms an attractive group with the surrounding houses. Other spires that come to mind are Bredon in Worcestershire, Brewood and especially Clifton Campville in Staffordshire, the two needle spires of St Alkmund and St Mary in Shrewsbury, and Worfield in Shropshire, and Astbury in Cheshire.

Finally, a couple of timber spires deserve to be noted – Fownhope in Herefordshire and Cleobury Mortimer (pl. 77), in Shropshire. Both are shingled.

Furnishings. Among post-Norman furnishings there are the font at Acton Burnell, the stalls and misericords at Nantwich, and two of the finest displays of stained glass in the country at Great Malvern and St Mary, Shrewsbury. The glass in the former is fifteenth century, but, as noted above, some of the glass at St Mary's is earlier and much of it comes from continental sources. These two churches show the tremendous importance of this form of decoration to a mediaeval church. Ludlow also has quite a lot of original glass but it is much restored. Herefordshire has much early fourteenth-century glass, notably the outstanding east window at Eaton Bishop. Other fourteenth-century glass can be seen at a number of Worcestershire churches, notably Kempsey, Birtsmorton, Bredon and Kyre Wyard. Great Malvern and Ludlow have fine sets of stalls with enchanting misericords, such as four rats hanging a cat at Great Malvern and an ale-wife carried off by a demon at Ludlow. The door-knocker at Dormington, in the same county, already mentioned, is a fine piece of Norman work, at the same time looking remarkably like a chihuahua!

Building materials and the economic state. One material above all others predominates in this region. Herefordshire, Warwickshire and most of Worcestershire are almost wholly situated on red sandstone, while Staffordshire, Shropshire and Cheshire, although overlaid with coal in Staffordshire and glacial clay in Cheshire and north Shropshire, all have a foundation of this stone. Except in Herefordshire, it dates from the Triassic and Permian series and is, therefore, about 180 to 270 million years old. The texture and often pink hue of the churches perfectly accord with the well-favoured countryside, thickly timbered and frequently landscaped into beautiful parks.

Sandstone is far and away the principal building stone of the west Midlands. Unfortunately, it is notoriously unreliable. It flakes and crumbles, and nowhere is this brought home more forcibly than in Sir George Gilbert Scott's reports on Chester Cathedral: 'the external stonework was so horribly and lamentably decayed as to reduce it to a mere wreck, like a mouldering sandstone cliff'. Carved details, both here and at other major buildings like Worcester Cathedral, just weathered and fell away. The result is that there is more, and let us admit, necessary Victorian restoration than in almost any other region. The patina of old age has disappeared under smooth refacing and greatly diminishes the visual pleasure of the buildings affected. The tower of the parish church of Waverton (pl. 85), near Chester, is a pleasant Perpendicular example with a nineteenth-century recessed pyramid roof, although the whole looks Victorian.

Fortunately not all the red sandstones wear so badly, and not all are red or pink. In Staffordshire, the colour is often yellow and at Gawsworth in Cheshire, a rather dirty ochre. Staffordshire has a much more resistant stone at Hollington, near Uttoxeter, which, as mentioned in Chapter 2, was selected by Sir Basil Spence for the new Coventry Cathedral. The fragments of quartz in its composition give it a slight sparkle. This stone was also used at Ludlow. In addition, Shropshire has red and white Grinshill sandstone, both of which are to be seen at Shrewsbury. Herefordshire has the more ancient old red sandstone of the Devonian system. This is harder but liable to split. Fortunately a particularly good variety was used at Kilpeck (pl. 81) so we can still enjoy the rich work of the period. Elsewhere, as near the Clee Hills in Shropshire, it can be soft.

There are, of course, other building materials. Towards the east of Cheshire, materials from the carboniferous formations were quarried, including millstone grit which is still in a satisfactory state at Astbury church (pl. 75). Throughout the mediaeval period, Cheshire was a good county for timber, as shown by the black-and-white magpie work (notably at Little Moreton Hall) for which not only Cheshire but Shropshire, Herefordshire and Worcestershire are famous. Complete churches in this material are to be seen at Marton and Lower Peover (excluding the tower) in Cheshire, Melverley and Halston in Shropshire and Besford in Worcestershire.

Warwickshire, although in the north a sandstone county, has both oolitic and lias limestones in the south. The oolite is a lovely creamy stone and the lias is Hornton stone of varying hues which in the south-east becomes an attractive light brown. Long Compton, with its strange lych-gate (a two-storeyed cottage with the ground floor removed) and Tredington are two of the churches which owe much to this material. Nearby Brailes (pl. 87) uses other materials, including brick, in the 110-foot Perpendicular tower. Worcestershire is mainly a brick county, although sandstone and the blue lias, both rather untrustworthy, are the prevailing materials for churches in the south-east. Those who know Broadway may object that this is made of the best limestone, but it is only just in the county and is by no means typical. The south of Shropshire has a broad range of old rocks, although it is usually only sandstone and more rarely limestone, which is suitable for building. However, the stones, like Hoar Slabs, are of only local importance. Herefordshire has a number of local stones, e.g. Silurian limestone near Woolhope, and carboniferous limestone and sandstone in the south-east, but four-fifths of the county is Devonian old red sandstone which, combined with glacial and river-borne silt and loam, produces the good red agricultural soil of the county and the overall pink colour of its churches. Finally, north-west Worcestershire has deposits of tufa, the strange sponge-like stone referred to in Chapter 2.

Economically, the whole area is good for cultivation and cattle-rearing. Worcestershire has been called 'the Surrey of the Midlands' and Cheshire 'the Surrey of south Lancashire'. In mediaeval times, there was a good average level of income, although nothing particularly exceptional. Weaving was generally practised, but on a small scale. In the fourteenth century Brailes grew into a bustling market town with a thriving watermill and an important wool trade. The Rylands sheep, one of the most famous of short-wooled breeds and one which produced exceptionally fine wool, was a source of money for Herefordshire churches. Cheshire derived earnings from its salt trade. Industry such as we know it today in the Birmingham and Stoke-on-Trent areas did not then exist and most activities were centred on the land.

The effects of this on churches must be considered in conjunction with the fact that sandstone was the main building material. The churches, Ludlow is a particular example, show the gradual growth from a small Norman rectangle to a large fifteenth-century church with clerestories and a stately tower. This general pattern is varied by the shapes and sizes of the churches, according to the number of chantry chapels required by the guilds and the absence, or not, of aisles. Perhaps no other part of England has so many churches with every mediaeval style represented, which makes it difficult to discover how and when the change from one style to another took place. Gnosall in Staffordshire and Lapworth in Warwickshire are other examples of this gradual development of styles.

General. The west Midlands are full of diversity in their places of worship. The combination of timber and sandstone, whether old or new, makes a fascinating tapestry and there is little stereotyped building to be seen. One moment one sees, for example, the completely timber-framed church at Besford, and the next, only three miles away, the proud if mutilated sandstone abbey church at Pershore. Sandstone does, however, pull the regional character together and Herefordshire has a most distinctive local style with its unusual Scandinavian-Celto-Norman sculpture and its detached towers.

On the other hand, one cannot state that this or that period was the golden age for the region as a whole: for Anglo-Saxon, virtually nothing; for Norman, Herefordshire; for Early English, perhaps Staffordshire more than others; for Decorated, Staffordshire, and for Perpendicular, Cheshire and Warwickshire. If one continues to later centuries, there are few counties which have so much of the best Victorian work as Staffordshire, possibly to meet the demands of a growing population for more churches.

Elsewhere in the region, however, the Victorian hand has lain heavily on churches. The Scotts and other architects have had their determined way, often to save a building from the effects of the crumbling sandstone, but frequently with great detriment to the original atmosphere of the building and its style.

Industry has imprinted its grimy and sooty mark on much of the Midlands, and, at times, one feels that one will never emerge from the great conurbations of Birmingham, Walsall, Wolverhampton and West Bromwich, and, further north, Stoke-on-Trent and the Pottery towns. Herefordshire, on the other hand, is one of the most rural counties in the land with beautiful scenery and a rolling landscape, while southern Warwickshire is pure Cotswolds, and, in Staffordshire, some people say that the Peak areas west of the River Dove in their county are better even than the eastern parts in Derbyshire. Cheshire and Worcestershire also provide pleasant living for those who keep the wheels of industry turning in the nearby manufacturing areas.

10 CELT AND SAXON

(CORNWALL, DEVONSHIRE, DORSET, GLOUCESTERSHIRE AND SOMERSET)

The south-western part of England was the last stronghold of the British in their struggle with the Saxons. Nowhere else in England are we made more conscious of Celtic influence than in Cornwall. The dedications of the churches soon make one aware of the differences between this county and the rest of England and, at a time when other parts were living through what is known as the Dark Ages, Cornwall was relatively civilized. Hermits came over from Ireland in the fifth and sixth centuries and set up cells from which Christianity was spread. If Sussex was the last county to be evangelized (see Chapter 4), Cornwall was the first.

Christians in the peninsula resented the coming of the Anglo-Saxons with their Roman forms of worship, and it was not until the subjugation of the county by King Athelstan in 936 that the fusion of the British and Anglo-Saxon churches was effected.

Cornwall seems to have drawn in Celts from Devon, for when the Saxons arrived in that county there is reason to believe that they found it denuded of people, and yet they do not appear to have settled in any number themselves. One finds, in consequence, a curious lack of both Celtic and Saxon traces.

Somerset was overrun in three stages, the final blow being struck by King Ina, who reigned from 688 to 726 and forced the British king, Geraint, to retire into Devon and Cornwall. Dorset, however, was able to make use of the elaborate Iron Age hill-forts which had been strengthened by the Romans to hold the invaders at bay. The legendary King Arthur was even reputed to have defeated them in battle. By the time the Saxons did break through, they were more civilized and the two peoples lived together without submerging one another, so that the county has retained more of its original stock than other parts.

The extent of the Saxons' penetration in Gloucestershire is not clearly known. They appear to have settled in the river valleys and especially in the Severn Vale where Deerhurst remains the most important memorial to their presence. Hwicce, one of the kingdoms of the Heptarchy, was spread out along the valleys of the Severn and Avon, and it is interesting to record that Ebba, daughter of Eanfrith, King of Hwicce in the seventh century, was yet another example of a woman of royal blood preparing the path for Christianity. When she married Ethelwach, a pagan king, she had a Christian priest with her and lived to see her husband become Christian, before he was killed in battle.

After Wiltshire, there is no county in England so rich in prehistoric remains as Cornwall. Many circles, built of the readily available granite, go back to the Early Bronze Age (1600 BC). The Nine Maidens at Zennor and the Hurlers at St Cleer are well-known stone circles which probably date from this period. Dolmens, with large capstones called 'quoits', are found at the extreme end of the peninsula and there is another of these megalithic chambers near St Cleer.

Anglo-Saxon. It is, therefore, not surprising that there are no substantial Saxon memorials in Cornwall and Devon but, more remarkably, even in Somerset there are few. In Dorset there are more, but only in Gloucestershire does one come across a major building.

In Cornwall, the well-known oratory of St Piran near Newquay is an evocative reminder of the early saints. This little, single-windowed cell, which was once buried in the sands, may have been the dwelling of a disciple of St Patrick who helped to convert Cornwall in the sixth and seventh centuries. It is the earliest Christian building in the southwest of England and one of the oldest anywhere in the country. The only other tangible remains of the Irish mission are the numerous crosses, mostly of the wheel type, of which the largest is at Mawgan-in-Pydar, also near Newquay.

Dorset offers tantalizing remains of a large church at Sherborne, consisting of rough masonry in the west wall and a doorway, and hints at other churches. Melbury Bubb has a font – probably part of a cross-shaft upside down – and, at Stinsford and Winterbourne Steepleton, there are two notable pieces of sculpture, the former unfortunately defaced, but the latter still very lively. Milborne Port, which is just inside Somerset on the Dorset border, is a rare example of a church which shows both Saxon and Norman work. Here Saxon pilaster decoration and Norman windows appear alongside one another in the tall and narrow chancel, typical of Saxon architecture.

Deerhurst, in Gloucestershire, has a Saxon building which ranks with Brixworth, Wing and Great Paxton. It was the most important religious centre in the kingdom of Hwicce and was a priory church. Here Edmund Ironside and Canute met when the boundaries between the Danes and Saxons were again defined. The nave and west wall may date to the early ninth century. The building is full of the most interesting Saxon remains, including numerous doorways, a chancel arch, sculpture of advanced design and fascinating animal heads including the exciting label-stop (see Glossary), *c.* 804, which is reminiscent of the figureheads of Scandinavian warships. In addition, this church has the finest Saxon font in the country. Dated as ninth century it is carved with the Celtic trumpet spiral, bordered with the vine scroll, a motif of Northumbria. This precious furnishing was found in a farmhouse nearby where it was used as a washtub! A double triangular-headed window looks out on to the nave from the upper stages of the tower, which itself is plain and the work of many different building programmes, with much herring-bone masonry incorporated.

But this is not all at Deerhurst. A discovery of great importance was made in 1885 when an adjacent half-timbered house was found to contain a complete, small late Saxon church. An inscribed stone found in a field nearby, and now in the Ashmolean Museum, Oxford, records that the church was consecrated in 1056 by Odda, cousin of Edward the Confessor, as a mortuary chapel for himself. Like Bradford-on-Avon in Wiltshire, the building was used purely for domestic purposes until, during repairs, a round window was found under the plaster. The mutilated chancel arch had been divided into two to make an upper floor, and the nave converted into a kitchen. As Escomb in County Durham was also revealed in the nineteenth century, three of the most exciting discoveries of small Saxon churches have been made in comparatively recent times. Are there more waiting to be found?

The church of the Holy Rood at Daglingworth, near Cirencester, has many traces of Saxon work, although much obscured by a rather thoroughgoing Victorian restoration. However, the arch over the south doorway with a fine Saxon sundial above it is pre-Conquest, and there are three tablets of Saxon sculpture inside, which, although naive in form and showing little appreciation of human proportions, are, as

David Verey rightly says, 'crude but inspired'. As with the Barnack figure of Christ, there is reason to believe that this is another attempt by the Normans to discredit anything Saxon, for the sculptures were found facing inwards in the jambs of the chancel arch. They represent the Crucifixion, St Peter holding the key, and Christ seated in an attitude of benediction.

Norman. One of the richest areas of the country in Norman times was the Cotswold Plateau. The reasons given by Verey are extremely interesting. He points out that this area had the finest sheep-runs and the best sheep of those days, in addition to which the roads left by the Romans facilitated distribution of the wool. The first wool-merchants' guild was actually started in Burford, Oxfordshire, 1080. He also comments that, for the country as a whole, England enjoyed a monopoly of the wool trade for many years, owing to the absence of wolves and the consequent safety of the sheep.

The result of this in terms of architecture is that there is hardly a Cotswold church that does not have traces of Norman work and many are complete Norman structures. They provide one of the happiest hunting-grounds for small twelfth-century village churches in the country. Some are without windows in the east end, possibly a relic from the days when churches had a defensive role; many have vaulted chancels (for example, Avening, which also has a vaulted crossing and spirally decorated jambs, reminiscent of Durham, in the north doorway); tympana and fonts abound, many of high sculptural merit.

Fonts will be referred to later, but, among tympana, that at Elkstone, north-east of Stroud, depicting Christ in Majesty, is the outstanding example. However, this Cotswold church has other attractions. It has a vaulted chancel, tower arches with much chevron ornamentation and a corbel-table preserved on the south side, all from the Norman period. Sculptured tympana are mainly to be found in the Cotswold area of Gloucestershire and, of the ten churches so decorated, Quenington has two examples. In the part of the county adjacent to Herefordshire, there are echoes of the Herefordshire school, notably the St George and Dragon at Ruardean.

Among the larger churches, Bishop's Cleeve has a Norman west front and transepts. This, however, is small in size compared with Tewkesbury Abbey, Gloucestershire's major Norman non-cathedral building. This is architecture on the grand scale – a veritable Norman masterpiece. Tewkesbury Abbey, founded as a Benedictine abbey not long after the Conquest and built mainly in the first quarter of the twelfth century, is larger than sixteen English cathedrals and is much more of a complete Norman building than Gloucester Cathedral, although both are distinguished by tall, massive, cylindrical columns in the nave arcades. Verey rates the magnificent central tower of Tewkesbury and its outstanding western arch as 'two of the noblest works of the period in all England'.

After this, the collegiate church of Wimborne – one of the few still called a minster – is the next most important twelfth-century building in the region but the impact is considerably less. It has a fine crossing tower; this competes, however, with the western tower, and the greensand stone and brown conglomerate of which it is built makes a rather unattractive mixture. Inside the impression is more agreeable, and the late twelfth-century nave with round piers rising to pointed arches is a major Norman arcade. The Minster occupies a prominent position in the centre of this small town.

Perhaps the next most considerable twelfth-century church in the region is St Germans in Cornwall. It shows many signs of its importance from the time when it was a priory of Augustinian Canons. Earlier, it was a cathedral but, even before the Conquest, it was merged with Crediton, Devon, into the new see of Exeter. (It is perhaps significant of the tenuous hold of the Saxons on Cornwall that the see of St Germans was only just within the confines of the county.) The church has the rare Norman feature of twin west towers (also found at Melbourne in Derbyshire) and a seven-order recessed portal under a pediment, made more distinctive by the fact that the portal is built of elvan, a rare stone – unfortunately much worn – of igneous character found only in Cornwall. Two bays of the arcade also remain from Norman times.

Neither Devonshire nor Somerset has anything on this scale. Milborne Port, in Somerset, was clearly at one time an important Norman church with crossing tower and transepts. But perhaps the most rewarding building in the county is Compton Martin, near the great lake of Blagdon which supplies Bristol with water, for this has a nave extraordinarily like that at Pittington, near Durham, with spiral decoration in relief on the piers. Stogursey has an interesting early Norman crossing and an elaborate late Norman chancel; Stoke-sub-Hamdon also has much work of that period. Numerically, there is much to see in Somerset – plenty of doorways, arches and fonts – but nothing of especial interest.

Bristol, which is a separate administrative county, has two churches, St James and All Saints, which have twelfth-century features. St James has intersecting blind arcading on the west front, a regional characteristic but found also in Wimborne tower, Dorset, and the very unusual feature of a rose window. All Saints has an attractive Norman arcade.

Apart from fonts the main Devonshire contributions for this period are towers. Sidbury has a Norman tower with the exceptional feature of an early vault. It is a west tower and this is the usual position, but, unlike some of the massive examples in the south-east, the Devonshire ones tend to be contracted and narrower than the nave. There are few crossing towers, as in Wiltshire and Dorset. Ottery St Mary (pl. 102) has transeptal towers, undoubtedly derived from the celebrated pair at Exeter Cathedral.

Nothing has been said about the smaller twelfth-century churches of Cornwall and Dorset. Tintagel is a typical plain village church with no transepts or aisles and a simple tower. Morwenstow has a partially twelfth-century arcade, the remainder being in the Early English and Perpendicular styles, an unusual combination of Norman and two Gothic forms. Dorset has two gems. Studland, near Swanage, is an uncommonly authentic village church of the first half of the twelfth century with a vaulted chancel and crossing, and Winterborne Tomson (pl. 97) is a charming example of a single-celled church of the same century with apse. It was fitted up in the eighteenth century with Georgian furnishings, but later became disused until restored in memory of the great Dorset novelist, Thomas Hardy.

There remain fonts. When Norman churches were later altered in favour of the new Gothic styles, fonts were often retained, possibly because it was felt that they still adequately fulfilled their purpose or perhaps because they were difficult to discard. More than 1,000 survive throughout the country. Of these, a very large proportion are in the south-west – 150 in Somerset, over 100 in each of Devonshire and Cornwall, at least 60 in Gloucestershire and probably a similar number in Dorset. One can only mention a few, and the Cornish types have already been mentioned in Chapter 1.

No less than nine of the Gloucestershire survivors are lead fonts, six Norman and three later, a very high proportion of the country's total of thirty or more. Of stone fonts, the outstanding example is the virtues and vices font at Southrop (see also Stanton Fitzwarren in Wiltshire) which depicts armoured women (the virtues) trampling on the vices. The names of both groups are carved in Latin but those of the vices are backwards. The church and the blindfolded figure of the synagogue are also shown, which would seem to indicate French influence (for instance, the west front of Strasbourg Cathedral). Lullington is the most elaborate font in Somerset and Churchstanton, in the same county, is of the Cornish type but the heads at the corners have never been carved. Luppitt in Devon is known for the strange vigorous carving on its font which has been variously interpreted, one theory being that the double-headed monster represents the evil of duplicity. Curious barbaric figures of another kind are seen at Toller Fratrum in Dorset. At St Mary, Wareham in Dorset, is the only hexagonal lead font in England. This has twelve figures under arches and delicately opens outwards towards the top. The church was substantially rebuilt in the 1840s on 'the grounds that the oratorical qualities of the then rector deserved a better setting'. But perhaps the best font in Dorset is at Stoke Abbott.

Early English. Except in Gloucestershire, the Early English representation is slight throughout the region, although, in Wells Cathedral, there is the first clear indication of an unreserved acceptance of the new style. Glastonbury Abbey was also rebuilt in this style after a serious fire and, as this was generally regarded as the premier monastic establishment in England, it is perhaps surprising that there is not more thirteenth-century work in Somerset. The explanation probably lies in what A. K. Wickham calls 'the passion for church building', which lasted two hundred years and transformed existing buildings or swept them away to be rebuilt in the new Perpendicular style. In Somerset this is particularly evident, for, apart from a few arcades, such as those at Queen Charlton, some work by Wells Cathedral masons at the churches of St Cuthbert at Wells and Wedmore, and porches like that at Tickenham, there is very little to be seen. There are, however, a number of stone bellcotes.

Neither is Dorset strong in thirteenth-century work. In this county, whatever the period, one tends to turn towards two of its major churches, Sherborne and Wimborne. In the Early English style there is the chancel of Wimborne and the Lady Chapel of Sherborne. For the later periods the third major church, Milton Abbey, must be included. This consists only of the eastern part – all that was rebuilt after the former Norman church was destroyed by fire. As is to be expected in the county of Purbeck, shafts are often used, as at St Martin, Wareham, and Stinsford, and there are a couple of typical chancels with lancets at Buckland Newton and Long Bredy. The best church for Early English, however, is Whitechurch Canonicorum which is mostly early thirteenth century and has the very rare feature of a complete stone shrine, this one dedicated to St Wite.

Cornwall has rather less. The nave of Crantock is thirteenth century and St Anthony-in-Roseland is a typical example of an early Gothic church without aisles or porches but with transepts and a crossing tower, in this case topped by a timber spire sheathed in lead. Devon is one of the most lightly represented counties of all and it would need a long search among the moors and combes to find even one group of mediaeval lancets. Work of this period is, in fact, confined almost entirely to the transepts of Branscombe Church (pl. 103).

Gloucestershire, however, has much more. There are many Cotswold churches with Early English chancels and the general trend to alter them in order to underline the division between clergy and laity is much in evidence. One church stands out above all others and that is not in the Cotswolds but in the Severn Vale. Berkeley, near the castle where Edward II met his horrible death, has an unusual west front, somewhat awkward but none the less effective in design, with five round-headed lancets above a wide central doorway flanked by blind arches and two massive buttresses. Internally, the nave arcade consists of seven bays decorated with finely and deeply cut stiff-leaf capitals.

As in Somerset the stone bellcote is a common sight in the Cotswolds, (for example Shipton Oliffe) as is the saddleback tower (see Chapter 3) of which Syde is one.

Decorated. Contrary to the two earlier periods, the Cotswolds are rather lean on Decorated. The style is mainly recognizable in the addition of transepts and sometimes in the enlarging of chancels. Decoration is sparingly used and sometimes arches are without capitals. Todenham, on the Warwickshire border, is the best example of a church in this part of Gloucestershire almost completely rebuilt in the fourteenth century. The tracery of the east window is especially noteworthy, as is the north arcade. As Todenham also has a fourteenth-century spire, the hallmark of the Decorated style, we have here a building which, both externally and internally, is a clear expression of the middle phase of Gothic as interpreted in a country parish.

The areas bordering on the Severn, however, are a better field for enjoying the more uninhibited manifestations of the style for there is much play with the favourite ball-flower ornament. Although not wool country, this factor was not so important in the early part of the fourteenth century and, in this area, the monastic influence of Gloucester and Tewkesbury still played a part. Newland, in the Forest of Dean (pl. 93) is, apart from those two monastic foundations, the *pièce de résistance*, so much so that it has earned for itself the appellation of 'Cathedral of the Forest'. Although restored in the nineteenth century, the effect of the wide, spacious interior is still striking; complemented with a noble, much-pinnacled tower and set in an ample churchyard, this is a fine parish church. Many people know it for its miner's brass. Of unknown origin, this mediaeval miner is shown in relief with hod and pick in his hands, and a candlestick in his mouth, the whole figure placed above a helmet of armour.

The choir of Tewkesbury Abbey with side chapels and sumptuous lierne vaulting is mainly fourteenth century and the same sophisticated form of vaulting was provided for the nave and transepts, so that this magnificent building – one of the finest parish churches in the southern half of England – is a remarkable blend, with its massive Norman nave piers and delicate Decorated vaulting. Standish, south of Gloucester, which is a complete fourteenth-century village church, has a memorable east window of five lights filled with reticulated tracery. Together with Newland, which has almost every form of Decorated tracery, we can see the whole range of this enjoyable contribution of the mid-Gothic style.

St Mary Redcliffe, Bristol, although mainly a Perpendicular church, has a most elaborately decorated inner doorway in the north porch.

Somerset, despite its later glories and perhaps because of them, is a county where the Decorated style is conspicuous by its absence. Generally, in this county, rectors left the chancel as it was while the congregations contributed generously to bigger and grander naves, for example the churches at Martock, South Petherton and Tintinhull. Sometimes transepts and towers remain, as at North Curry and Somerton; sometimes an aisle, for example Curry Rivel and Hemington; and at other times only the nave arcades, Shepton Mallet and Pilton.

In Devonshire, all that is best of the Decorated period is associated with one man – Bishop Grandisson, who ran the diocese for over forty years, from 1327 to 1369, which was the peak of this style. Under him, the exquisite nave of Exeter Cathedral was built, its superb roof the acme of perfection in fourteenth-century vaulting. He was also responsible for Devon's most notable Decorated church, Ottery St Mary (pl. 102), which he founded as a college. The chapel of St Blaise at Haccombe, a largely fourteenth-century building since reconditioned, was another consecrated by Grandisson. Bere Ferrers and Tawstock are other mainly fourteenth-century churches which have retained their Decorated character. On the whole, the new forms were applied with restraint in Devonshire and there is nothing of the full flowing tracery seen in other areas.

The intractability of Cornwall's granite limited the repertoire of shapes and decoration, especially in the later mediaeval period. However, exceptions are to be found in Fowey and Lostwithiel, the latter with a beautiful stone spire, which are interesting examples of fourteenth-century work not far away from one another. The nave arcades are without capitals, while they share with St Germans and Callington the local trait of clerestories starting below the points of the arches in the spandrels. St Ive, a delightfully complete village church, has a fine east window.

Dorset, like Devonshire, is restrained in the use of tracery and the best example is the south window of the south transept of Milton Abbey. Quite often, one comes across square-headed windows with ogee tracery. The most complete fourteenth-century church is Gussage All Saints in the north-east of the county, but the chancel was rebuilt in Victorian times.

Spires. It is not to be expected that in an area where there is so much emphasis on the Perpendicular style of architecture, that there would be many mediaeval stone spires of east Midlands quality. Nor, in fact, are there. In Dorset, there are only three, all dating from the fourteenth century: Iwerne Minster, Trent and Winterbourne Steepleton.

The most elaborate in Cornwall is Lostwithiel. Among the dozen or so others are St Enodoc, St Ewe, Rame, St Keverne and St Anthony-in-Roseland. Devon, as one would anticipate in such a large county, has a few more, but they are the exception rather than the rule.

Gloucestershire, however, has several scattered around the county. They have a regional flavour in that they are slender with a narrow base and roll-mouldings on the angles; Ruardean is particularly noteworthy. They are mostly of the Decorated period, although some, like Painswick, are later. Westbury-on-Severn's shingled spire surmounts a tower away from the church, which is thought to have been used as a watch-tower during border troubles. Somerset has sixteen spires, of which Congresbury is the most interesting.

Although we have become accustomed to finding a *chef-d'œuvre* among lesser works, the spire of St Mary Redcliffe in Bristol has still to be mentioned. Built in the first half of the fourteenth century and struck by lightning in the fifteenth, it was not rebuilt until the nineteenth century. With its abundant pinnacling, restrained spire-lights and soaring height, reaching to 292 feet, it is one of the most successful spire compositions in the land and is a worthy accompaniment to this noble church.

Perpendicular. Most of what has been described so far in this chapter is a run-up to what A. K. Wickham, in his charming book, *Churches of Somerset*, so aptly calls 'The Great Epoch'. In no other region does the Perpendicular style predominate to the same extent. Every one of the counties comprising the region has more fifteenth- and sixteenth-century architecture than of any other previous century; in Devonshire more than 90 per cent of all its pre-Reformation work is of this period. As in Suffolk, wool wealth led to extensive or complete rebuildings both in Somerset and Gloucestershire. Cornwall developed a most distinctive form of L-shape profile with tall tower and long, low lines which admirably suits the open and often moorland sweep of the county, in which the churches – built mainly of granite – frequently stand isolated and prominent. Windows are often square-headed, accentuating the effect. Nowhere, perhaps, has geology imprinted its mark so forcibly and imposed such a satisfying rapport between man and nature. Clerestories are rare; their absence and the prolongation of the aisles to terminate at a point parallel with the east end of the chancel produces the three-gable east end, also seen in Kent. St Ives is exceptional in this county as having four gables.

One of the finest of Cornish buildings is Kilkhampton, built during the rectorship of John Greville, which lasted for over half the sixteenth century. The nave with its seven bays is especially fine. Of the same date is Probus which, in addition to having the finest tower in the county, possesses a stately interior. Altarnun (pl. 105) is another fine Perpendicular church standing up most effectively above the village. Its position graphically demonstrates the predominance of the mediaeval church in the life of a community and Altarnun is an interesting example of a place of worship built to glorify God rather than to accommodate large numbers, although in area the parish is the largest in the county.

The infrequency of clerestories carries on into Devonshire where there are only ten. These include Ottery St Mary (pl. 102) and Cullompton (pl. 100). Fifteenth- and sixteenth-century additions were mainly in the form of aisles to accommodate a chantry chapel or increased congregations, the chancels being already large enough. Arcades and window tracery follow a standard pattern and there is not much variety. The normal Devon church has no structural division between nave and chancel, the wagon roof runs continuously through the building and a wooden screen, extending right across nave and aisles, often takes the place of the chancel arch.

Perpendicular construction is found throughout Dorset. The period produced the best architecture in the county, but it is only outstanding at Sherborne where the first large scale fan-vault was built in 1450. Clerestories are again uncommon and the churches have a predominantly rural air. Aisles are wide and often battlemented throughout. Windows are uneventful except for the large west window and one in the south transept at Sherborne, but some churches have four-light windows as in the south chapel at Loders (pl. 98). Towers are squat and sturdy with boldly projecting stair-turrets, sometimes battlemented and with pinnacles.

Yeovil, which was completely rebuilt at the end of the fourteenth century, ushered in the glorious Perpendicular era in Somerset. Along the course of the River Parrett, between this town and Bridgwater, lies a string of the best late mediaeval churches, although this is not the only part of the county in which to find them. Noble churches like Bruton (pl. 94) are to be found elsewhere.

Towers, roofs and screens are undoubtedly the highlights of the Somerset contribution to the fifteenth and sixteenth centuries. Of course, there are other items as well, but the Perpendicular churches of Somerset are smaller than those of East Anglia and give the impression of having been rebuilt with the gifts of successful merchants retiring to their native villages. Sometimes, as at Wrington and Evercreech, the parapets are elaborate and pierced with tracery; in other cases, as at Ile Abbots and Crowcombe, ornate aisles, often containing windows with cusped transoms, were added. Chancels, on the other hand, are often disappointingly small – no doubt due to the system where responsibility for this part was left to the rector (possibly a lay rector). Porches often took on much stateliness and at Mells, Doulting and Wellow there are examples of concave-sided gables.

Perhaps, apart from the Somerset towers and St Mary Redcliffe, Bristol, the richest field in the region for Perpendicular churches is Gloucestershire. As in the East Riding, there is a group of resplendent churches which are a striking testimony to the prosperity of the wool areas. Chipping Campden, Cirencester, Northleach, Fairford and Winchcombe owe much of their splendour to the munificence of rich wool-merchants – Grevel at Chipping Campden, Fortey at Northleach and Tame at Fairford – and, at Cirencester and Winchcombe, the former monastic owners. The abbey contributed the south porch at Cirencester, built at the end of the fifteenth century and the most magnificent in England. It was not handed over to the church until the eighteenth century, before that it was known as the Town Hall. It is three storeys high, three bays wide and three bays deep. The parishioners, however, were responsible for rebuilding the nave in the first quarter of the sixteenth century, and the arms and marks of the contributors are to be seen on the sides of the nave piers. In addition to other glories there is much stained glass and a pre-Reformation pulpit, of which there are several in Gloucestershire. But, for stained glass, the great display is at Fairford which, in the most complete set of fifteenth-century glass in England, depicts faith throughout the ages.

Northleach, Chipping Campden and Cirencester share the local trait of having a window above the chancel arch, although this also occurs at Tickhill in the West Riding. Winchcombe, on the other hand, has no chancel arch at all and is the least showy of the wool Gloucestershire churches, but, nevertheless, the large clerestory and interior spaciousness give an air of distinction set off externally by a splendid, gilded weathercock which came from St Mary Redcliffe, Bristol.

No doubt this great church could afford to part with it, for here we are at the very summit of mediaeval parish church architecture. Queen

Elizabeth I described it as 'the fairest, goodliest, and most famous parish church in England', probably an even greater compliment in her day than in ours. It typifies architecture's new emphasis in the later Middle Ages. Now it was the parish church, not the cathedral or monastery, upon which the masons concentrated their utmost resources. The glory of St Mary Redcliffe is the lofty and airy interior and, outside, the fourteenth-century spire and the elaborate parapeting, as well as the inner doorway of the north porch.

Towers. Many attempts have been made to classify the Somerset towers, usually on a largely geographical basis. One major division, which Pevsner uses, is whether the parts rising above the roof-line of the nave are subdivided horizontally or form one complete stage. The latter category, though by no means uniform, is based upon the towers of Wells Cathedral and is distinguished by the fact that the tracery of the two windows above is carried down so as to form blind panels in the lower portion. The lights of the windows are separated by bold shafts which also continue downwards. St Cuthbert's, Wells, Evercreech and Wrington have pinnacles, while Batcombe (pl. 92) has a parapet but no pinnacles.

Wickham uses this group too, but also distinguishes others: the West Mendip group, East Mendip group, south Somerset group and Taunton group.

The West Mendip group may well be based upon the tower of Shepton Mallet. Churches in this group have three windows in the top stage, of which the centre one is pierced for the sound of the bells; they have straight parapets, shallow buttresses and are built of a grey stone. Axbridge, Banwell, Bleadon, Brent Knoll, Cheddar, Weare and Winscombe are examples. They are early and, although enjoyable, they fall short of the more mature Somerset towers which came later. Shepton Mallet was originally meant to have a spire, but it had only reached eight feet when it was realized that the tower was sufficient by itself.

The East Mendip group consists of Bruton (pl. 94), Leigh-on-Mendip and Mells. These are three of the finest towers in the county. They also have triple windows in the top stage, each being pierced for the sound of the bells; they are battlemented and there are many niches for statues.

In the South Somerset group the churches each have a tall window extending through both upper stages and divided by a thick, ornamented transom. Below is a large space without windows. There is a pinnacle near each corner but not, except at Hinton St George, on the corner as in Dorset at Fordington and Piddletrenthide. Examples include Norton-sub-Hamdon and Crewkerne as well as Hinton St George, all three being built of golden-coloured Ham Hill stone.

Finally, there is a group probably built by masons from Taunton which is perhaps the most outstanding. They are characterized by harmony of proportion, wealth and delicacy of detail, the number of pinnacles, frequency of niches and by having two windows in the top storey. North Petherton (pl. 96), is one of this group. It is built of blue lias and Ham Hill stone, as is Ile Abbots, which still retains most of its original statues in the niches. Kingsbury, another church in this group, is built entirely of Ham Hill, while Bishop's Lydeard and the two rebuilt Taunton towers are constructed of red sandstone. Others are Staple Fitzpaine, Kingston St Mary and Huish Episcopi. Wickham gives the crown in this group to three of the smaller towers, Ile Abbots, Staple Fitzpaine and Kingston St Mary, which he says are 'among the greatest masterpieces of English architecture'.

Among other notable Somerset towers are: Chewton Mendip, which has similar sculpture on its west face to that at Batcombe, and was probably designed by the same mason; Ilminster, which, though much later, was obviously inspired by the central tower of Wells Cathedral; St John's, Glastonbury, which has affinities with the Gloucestershire towers and which Wickham generously regards as a 'handsome stranger in our midst'; and Weston Zoyland. These, together with the others already mentioned, include most of the best towers; hardly one is without its individual touches and together they make a group of noble towers which Lawrence Jones regards as the finest in the world.

The best Gloucestershire towers – Gloucester Cathedral, Northleach, Chipping Campden, Fairford, Yate and Thornbury – have a character all their own with diagonal instead of set-back buttresses (see Chapter 1) and string-courses continuing round the buttresses and making a strong horizontal line. There is much blind panelling which, in some cases, can be excessive. Bristol is especially rich in good towers, notably St Stephen's, and in the environs there are Chipping Sodbury and Bitton. Perpendicular towers were built all over the county and, if the general average is not as high as in Somerset, the main fabrics may well be deemed finer.

Devonshire, in addition to the outstanding example at Chittle-hampton, has many dignified towers, such as the favourite picture-postcard example at Widecombe-in-the-Moor. However, because of the more intractable nature of the materials (old sandstone, carboniferous limestone and granite) of which they were built, they are more austere and have less adornment. There are often large, bare spaces of wall with only one window in the top stage. Many, such as Talaton (pl. 99), have stair-turrets continuing above the parapet and a number in the south, for example, Harberton, Ipplepen, Torbryan, have a peculiarly local feature in that the turrets are placed in the middle of one side. Among the more notable Devonshire towers one must list Totnes, Cullompton (pl. 100) and Kenton, all of bright red sandstone, and South Molton and Hartland.

In Cornwall the towers of Fowey and St Austell stand out for special mention. Probus, the best, has already been highlighted and Kilk-hampton is notable. Landewednack (pl. 104), apart from being the most southerly in England, is made of the local serpentine stone, giving it a black and greenish hue.

The Dorset characteristic of three pinnacles at the corners on Ford-ington and Piddletrenthide towers has been mentioned. Another of this type is St Peter, Dorchester. Piddletrenthide is constructed of Pur-beck while the other two are of Portland stone, all three having dressings of a material of Ham Hill character. Sherborne and Milton, which are very similar, are central towers of only one stage above the roof-line. There remains Charminster, a late example with square-headed win-dows, lower and broader than the others in the Dorchester region and, best of all, Beaminster – an ambitious construction, no doubt trying to vie with Somerset.

Roofs and screens. The typical roof of the West Country is the wagon or barrel roof, either open or plastered, and occasionally boarded over, in which the rafters have curved instead of arched braces, creating, when plastered over, the effect of the covering of a wagon. This roof is the appropriate covering to the long, aisleless buildings of Devon and Cornwall and the low pitch accords with a region so predominantly Perpendicular.

In the eastern part of the county, we also find the low-pitched tie-beam roof with tracery above the beam and the flat roof, supported by cambered beams. With the exception of the pseudo hammer-beam example at Bere Regis, Dorset, quite the most splendid in the county, we do not meet with the hammer-beam type. Most are late Perpendicular of a period when steep-pitched roofs were no longer fashionable.

For once, Gloucestershire is in a minor key, but in the rest of the region there are many notable ones. Somerset has many excellent tie-beam roofs, as at Martock, Somerton, Evercreech, St Cuthbert's, Wells, Weston Zoyland and Leigh-on-Mendip. Shepton Mallet has one of the wagon type which is particularly fine. This supreme example of a completely panelled roof has 350 panels, each of which is differently designed. It is the same with the 300 bosses, which are nailed to and do not support the panels.

For screens, Devonshire is justifiably famous. They often stretch across nave and aisles and take the place of the chancel arch. Frequently coved with ribs, shaped into fan-vault patterns and richly carved, the majority still coloured and gilt, they are more sumptuous in many ways than the more restrained East Anglian type, but not necessarily more beautiful as works of art and with painting of lesser quality on the panels. Among numerous examples one might mention Atherington – the only one to retain its rood-loft – Bradninch, Chulmleigh, Cullompton, St Saviour's, Dartmouth, Hartland, Plymtree, Swimbridge and Lapford. The figure paintings are stumpier than in East Anglia.

Cornwall has lost many wooden screens, but the grace and skill of the mediaeval carpenter is still to be enjoyed in the bench-ends. The county is an unusual blend of high churchmanship and nonconformity and the former has led to the restoring of roods in more than one church in comparatively recent times. Blisland and Mullion are two examples of this.

Somerset has examples of both the Devonshire fan-vaulted type and of a square-headed type of Midlands extraction. The former is designed to go with a chancel arch so that the rood-screen is higher, as the arch dictates, than the aisle screens. Wickham finds this less 'aesthetically disturbing' than the screen stretching in an unbroken line right across. His preference is for Long Sutton, but others of note are Banwell, Mine-head and, perhaps the best, Dunster. This, together with Minehead, is of the Devon type.

Gloucestershire has lost most of its screens and there is little to see. Dorset has a number of stone screens, as at Nether Compton, as well as some wooden ones, including a very fine example of the Devon type at Trent.

Furnishings. In a region so rich, it would require much space for even the briefest of surveys. The exceptionally comprehensive display of stained glass at Fairford has been mentioned. This may have been designed by the glazier responsible for the glass of the Henry vii Chapel at Westminster Abbey in London, alas now nearly all disappeared. One cannot omit, however, the unusually extensive fifteenth- and early sixteenth-century glass at St Neot, Cornwall, and there is a superb survival of mid-fourteenth-century glass in the clerestory of the presbytery at Tewkesbury Abbey, and much late fifteenth-century work in the east window of Cirencester.

A particular feature is the number of pre-Reformation pulpits, both of stone and of wood, that remain in this region. Despite the crudity of some of the decoration of the wooden ones, the stone ones are often beautifully proportioned and generally octagonal in shape, long and narrow, and usually supported on a slender 'wineglass' stem. Of a probably unique type are the wooden ones at Long Sutton, Somerset and Chivelstone, Devonshire. The former has sixteen sides, each bearing the carved figure (renewed) of a saint, and at Chivelstone the pulpit is hollowed out of a single large block of oak. Trull, in Somerset, has its original carved figures of the Four Latin Doctors and St John the Evangelist. Apparently these have survived because they were buried for many years.

Mediaeval pulpits of stone number about sixty, and they are most common in Somerset, Gloucestershire and Devon. Examples are Banwell in Somerset, Northleach in Gloucestershire and Harberton. The last, like others in Devon, is coloured.

Benches, most of which date from the end of the mediaeval era when more attention was placed on the sermon, and therefore, greater comfort needed, are mostly square-ended and only occasionally have the poppy-heads so common in East Anglia. Notable ones are at Trent and Bradford Abbas in Dorset, East Budleigh and High Bickington in Devonshire, and Launcells in Cornwall. In western Somerset there is an entertaining group with country scenes – a dog seizing a rabbit by the tail at Monksilver, wrestlers and a carpenter at Lyng, the famous fuller at Spaxton and the equally well-known windmill at Bishop's Lydeard. At Brent Knoll, three bench-ends depict the humorous satire of Reynard the Fox, who is disguised as a mitred abbot.

This is not a great region for wall-paintings. St Mary, Kempley in Gloucestershire, however, has examples from the twelfth century which are outstandingly beautiful, and Stoke Orchard in the same county has a complete set from the end of the century, depicting the life of St James of Compostela.

Brasses are notably deficient, except at Northleach, Gloucestershire, the reason probably being that the area was far removed from the continental source of the material used, latten (see Chapter 4).

There is the usual large complement of monuments, but this is a subject too wide to cover adequately in this book. Perhaps the best are the fourteenth-century monuments at Tewkesbury, but, although Dorset was the source of the Purbeck marble so much used for tombs, they are not especially noteworthy in this county, and the same must be said of Somerset.

Building materials and economic wealth. The eastern part of the region is favoured by being located at the south-western end of the great oolite crescent (see Chapter 2). This produces the matchless light golden colour of the Cotswold villages, the grey Doulting, and the honey-golden Bath stones, and the famous white Portland stones of Dorset. This great formation of limestone also provides the delightful stone tiles of Purbeck and Stonesfield, seen to such advantage in the village of Corfe Castle and city of Oxford respectively.

Oolitic limestones, however, are only the cream of a very complicated geological pattern ranging through the 500 million years of the span referred to in Chapter 2. There is plenty of young chalk in Dorset, largely composed of this material, as well as lias to the west of the oolite and then, further west, red sandstone. The lias embraces the golden Ham Hill stone which is such a feature of villages like Martock and Montacute and, when combined with blue lias, is part of the charm of Somerset towers like Ile Abbots and North Petherton.

Red sandstone is the major building material along the south coast of Devon from Torquay to Sidmouth and also up the valley of the Exe, and it is this which gives rise to the well-known red soil. But there are other stones, such as the older slate-grey Devonian sandstone formations and the so-called Culm materials (siliceous sandstone). There is even a little limestone around Beer in the south-east as well as chalk.

There remain the most characteristic materials of the extreme south-west – granite and slate-stone – together with a few curiosities of igneous origin such as elvan, catacleuse, polyphant and serpentine, the last being the main rock of the Lizard Peninsula and the material of the tower of Landewednack church (pl. 104). The prevailing tone of granite is silver-grey, not pink as in Aberdeen or in the Channel island of Jersey, but additional colour is provided by the more varied hues of slate-stone which comes in brown, grey and other colours. Despite the exuberant carving at Launceston church, witness to the Celtic love of decoration, granite does not yield readily to the chisel and sometimes, as at Altarnun, pier, base and capital are carved out of one block of stone, the funnel-shaped form of the capital being dictated by the material. Nevertheless, these stones, which are not used anywhere else in England on the same scale for the fabrics of churches, convey an unmistakable individuality to the places of worship of this part of the country.

At the beginning of the Perpendicular period, Somerset was one of the most important weaving centres in England, especially for broad-cloths. Gloucestershire, too, was a great wool county but, whereas in East Anglia most villages were prosperous as a result of this trade, the wealth in this western county tended to be concentrated in large centres such as Chipping Campden, Northleach and Fairford. This no doubt accounts for the number of Cotswold village churches which retain their Norman features from an earlier period of sheep plenty and which have not been rebuilt. In Devonshire, the signs of wool wealth are also localized, but the south aisle built by John Lane at Cullompton and the Dorset north aisle at Ottery St Mary with their sumptuous fan-vaults are clear indications of fifteenth-century prosperity which probably explains the very high proportion of Perpendicular work, despite the lack of clerestories, in mediaeval churches. Cornwall and Dorset were less affected by this source of income, but there were tin-mines in Corn-wall. Another mining activity was the extraction of lead in Somerset, which was probably the main source of this mineral for roofs and fonts. There was also no lack of good harbours.

General. We started in the extreme south-east, near to the continental source from which much of our architecture originated and we finish in the extreme south-west looking out to the lands which, in their turn, have been influenced by the styles that developed here. This south-west region is second only to East Anglia and Lincolnshire in the splendour of its parish church architecture and bows to no other region in the grace and dignity of its fifteenth-century towers. It is the nearest approach to the combination of great architecture with fine scenery and good building stone and we can see every variety of place of worship from the majestic St Mary Redcliffe, Bristol, to the tiny church at Culbone, Somerset, which is the smallest mediaeval parish church in England. Perhaps nowhere else is the regional stamp more clearly impressed or has man co-operated with nature to the same extent to produce beautiful churches in delightful settings, in a timeless harmony.

CONCLUSION

The regional pictures will have given some indication of the richness of England's heritage of mediaeval parish churches. It is probably reasonable to state that in no other country do so many ancient places of worship still bear witness to the paramount part they played in the life of the people. The church brought everyone together and all went through its doors. From the seventh century, when Archbishop Theodore of Canterbury encouraged lords of the manor to found parish churches, until the end of the Middle Ages, when rich merchants were prepared to devote part of their wealth to beautifying and enlarging these houses of God, craftsmen in stone and wood concentrated their skills on making them worthy places of worship.

As F. E. Howard has pointed out, the mediaeval builders had an unerring sense of proportion and feeling for scale, and seemed to know exactly what could be done with the means and materials at their disposal. There was a grace about almost everything they touched, probably helped by the fact that the designer was also the builder. Moreover, as life was short, the craftsmen were probably young men and their work reflects a youthful spirit.

Unfortunately, what we see today – enjoyable as it is – differs greatly from what existed before the Reformation and much beauty has been lost. Sixteenth- and seventeenth-century iconoclasm, eighteenth-century indifference and nineteenth-century insensitivity have taken their toll, especially of the furnishings. It is customary to look upon old churches as cool sanctuaries of grey stone. The mediaeval church was not at all like this, there was colour everywhere. The darkness did not matter, for the offices were conducted in Latin and most people could not read. Probably the only things which had real meaning for the congregations of those days were the sermon, the stained glass and the painted murals, from which they could obtain plain guidance about the life of Christ and its meaning for them. Hardship and hazard were never far away and the ordinary man wanted something which could bring joy and pleasure to his drab world. The wall-paintings and, above all, the vivid colours of the glass did this for him and must have created a sense of devotion, as he gazed up and saw how the light, which to the mediaeval mind was the source of all life, was converted into coloured pictures he could understand.

Alas, these beautiful achievements of the mediaeval craftsmen, together with statues and roods, became the particular butt of the Reformers, who associated them with all the mysticism and imagery of the Roman Church which they most disliked. First it was the statues, roods and wall-paintings which suffered, but the simplest way of effacing the offending murals was to lime-wash them over and they remained intact under the covering. At the beginning of Elizabeth's reign, it was the turn of the rood-lofts. This destruction was ostensibly directed against superstition, but in reality was a move against the popular church music played by an orchestra in the loft. Glass was only spared for a while because of the difficulty of making the building weather-proof. But the reprieve only lasted until the middle of the next century, when Oliver Cromwell and his followers made a determined onslaught on what they regarded as 'relics of idolatry' and any devotional aspect was condemned. How one would like to have taken colour photographs before all this happened!

It is arguable, however, whether even this wanton destruction was not exceeded in later centuries by the damage of neglect, bad restoration and poor taste. Restoration of glass, for example, was frequently carried out by inexperienced and insensitive hands – thick bars might be placed across the faces or figures, or pieces of glass from other windows inserted in a crazy patchwork. In other cases, mediaeval glass of merit might be replaced by product of inferior quality.

In the nineteenth century it was fashionable to expose stonework. This meant stripping off or 'skinning' the plaster so that the wall-paintings which still existed under the coating of lime-wash were destroyed for ever. An incalculable loss which means, in general, that however well preserved is the main body of a mediaeval church, we can never see it in its original form.

The present age is more sensitive to the beauty and artistic richness of what the mediaeval builder and craftsman created. A beautiful church is a source of pride to the town or village where it is situated.

Various trusts do valiant work in arousing national and local interest in this priceless heritage. The present danger lies in the passion for re-organization, for streamlining. It is conservatively estimated that between two and three thousand churches may be made redundant within the next ten or fifteen years. Some will be converted to other uses but it is hoped that most will be preserved.

Congregations may sometimes be small, but we should, perhaps, pause and consider our stewardship of this unique part of our heritage. Great church architecture inspires reverence. Generations to come may judge our claim to be civilized by the way we look after and preserve what is best from the past. Upon this can be built a future.

Location of Churches
*(Boundaries shown are those
prior to the 1974 changes.)*

THE COLOUR PLATES

1   Brown stone tower patched with brick, Ightham, Kent.

2　Sixteenth-century sandstone tower, Seal, Kent.

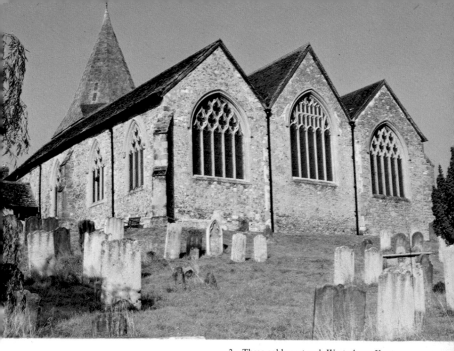

3 Three gable east end, Westerham, Kent.

4 The steep, catslide roof, Amberley, Sussex.

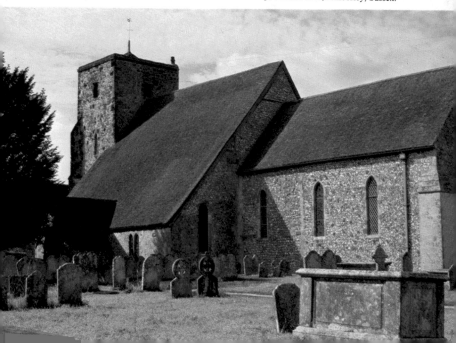

5   Late Norman tower, Climping, Sussex.

6   Perpendicular tower topped by a shingled timber spire, West Hoathly, Sussex.

7 Mid 12th century Norman village church, Pyrford, Surrey.

8 The simple 13th century downland church at Didling, Sussex.

9   Tower and cupola, Harmondsworth, Middlesex.

10 Timber tower at Margaretting, Essex.

11   Late mediaeval brick tower, Ingatestone, Essex.

12 South porch of Tudor brick. Sandon. Essex.

13   The soaring lead-sheathed timber tower at Hemel Hempstead, Hertfordshire.

14 Shingled spirelet, Aldenham church, Hertfordshire.

15 The epitome of Early English architecture, Felmersham, Bedfordshire.

16 & 17 Two village churches that combine the styles of the 13th and
14th centuries, *top* Shelton, Bedfordshire and *below* Compton
Beauchamp, Berkshire.

18   Stately Chiltern church, Ivinghoe, Buckinghamshire.

19   The dominating position of Edlesborough church, Buckinghamshire.

20 Mid Perpendicular church, almost unchanged since it was built, Minster Lovell, Oxfordshire.

21 Decorated capital of human heads with intertwined arms, Hampton Poyle, Oxfordshire.

22 The Stapleton monument, Rotherfield Greys, Oxfordshire.

23 The Saracen, a monument at Lingfield, Surrey.

24   The mediaeval manor church, Stanton Harcourt, Oxfordshire.

25 Baroque monument to the Harcourt family, Stanton Harcourt.

26   Box-like bellcote with crocketed spirelet, Great Chalfield, Wiltshire.

27   The chancel screen, Petersfield, Hampshire.

28   A church with much Saxon work, Breamore, Hampshire.

29   Village church of the 13th century, East Wellow, Hampshire.

30   Thames-side church, Bisham, Berkshire.

31   Perpendicular tower with polygonal turrets and clerestory, Hasling- field, Cambridgeshire.

32 & 33 Two of Suffolk's finest churches, examples of the wealth brought to the region by the mediaeval wool trade, *top* Lavenham and *below* Long Melford.

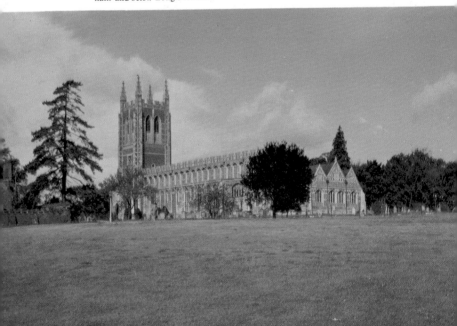

34   The round tower at South Pickenham, Norfolk.

35   East Anglian thatch, Thurton, Norfolk.

36   Magnificent Perpendicular architecture, Southwold, Suffolk.

37   The fine detached tower, West Walton, Norfolk.

38   Village church of the late 14th century, Walpole St Peter, Norfolk.

39   Early Perpendicular, Swanton Morley, Norfolk.

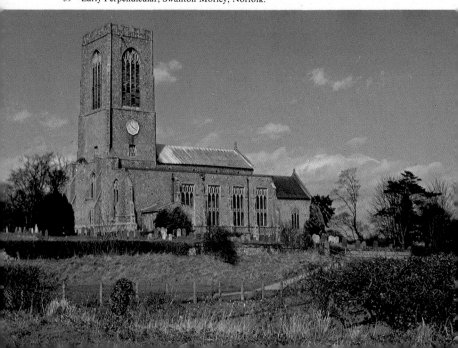

40 Mediaeval rood-screen and loft, with fragments of a mural above,
Attleborough, Norfolk.

41 The great hammerbeam roof, Cawston, Norfolk.

42 West end and tower built 1440–80, Tattershall, Lincolnshire.

43 Perpendicular clerestory added to a Decorated church, Gedney, Lincolnshire.

44 Saxon chancel arch, Stow, Lincolnshire.

45　Broach spire of the mid 14th century, Spaldwick, Huntingdonshire.

46   Tall 14th century tower and short stone spire, Empingham, Rutland.

47   The great Norman chancel arch, Tickencote, Rutland.

48   Ironstone 13th and 14th century church, Kirby Bellars, Leicestershire.

49 Tower and broach spire of the 13th and 14th centuries, Ketton, Rutland.

50   Norman south door with re-used Roman tiles, Brixworth, Northamptonshire.

51 South-east view of the round-naved church of Holy Sepulchre, Northampton.

52   Predominantly 13th century village church, Teversal, Nottinghamshire.

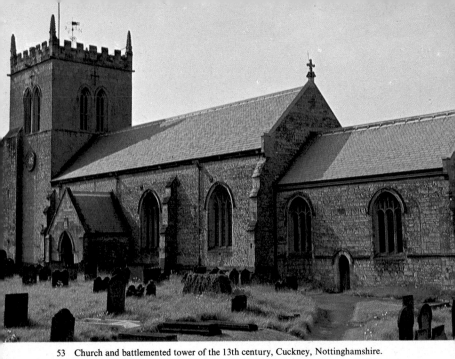

53 Church and battlemented tower of the 13th century, Cuckney, Nottinghamshire.

54 Church of the 12th century with Saxon tower, Carlton-in-Lindrick, Nottinghamshire.

55 Early 16th century tower of orange lias and grey oolite, Whiston, Northamptonshire.

56 Stately town church incorporating the styles of many periods, Bakewell, Derbyshire.

57 Perpendicular ashlar faced tower and spire, Bonsall, Derbyshire.

58 Another fine town church, Wirksworth, Derbyshire.

59 'The Cathedral of the Peak', Tideswell, Derbyshire.

60 Norman village church, Isel, Cumberland.

61 The cliffside church of Norman origin at Whitby, Yorkshire.

62   Re-built Norman tower, Seamer, Yorkshire.

63   'One-third tower, two-thirds spire', Hemingbrough, Yorkshire.

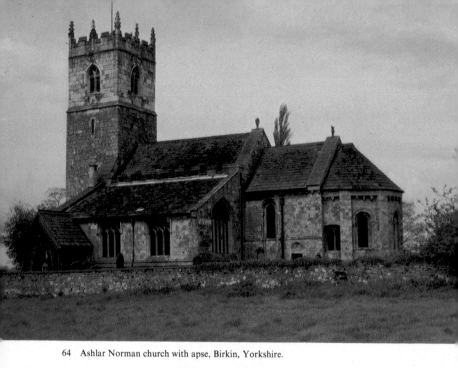

64 Ashlar Norman church with apse, Birkin, Yorkshire.

65 Castle and church, West Tanfield, Yorkshire.

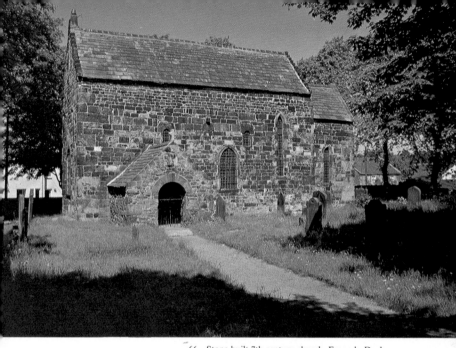

66   Stone built 7th century church, Escomb, Durham.

67   A church of all periods, Staindrop, Durham.

68   The Saxon tower at Corbridge, Northumberland.

69 Early English architecture with typical lancet windows, Haltwhistle, Northumberland.

70   West end of the late 13th century church, Lanercost, Cumberland.

71   Nave of the 15th century with a 17th century upper arch, Grasmere, Westmorland.

72 Late 12th century body and early 16th century tower, Beetham,
Westmorland.

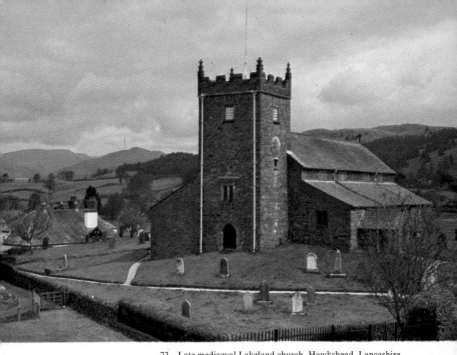

73   Late mediaeval Lakeland church, Hawkshead, Lancashire.

74   The massive east window typical of the Perpendicular style, Cartmel Priory, Lancashire.

75 Clerestory windows set in walls of millstone grit, Astbury, Cheshire.

76 Midland honey-coloured tower and pinnacled parapet, Kineton, Warwickshire.

77 Twisted shingled spire, Cleobury Mortimer, Shropshire.

78 & 79   Two mediaeval castles with their churches, *top* Stokesay, Shropshire and *below* Croft, Herefordshire.

80   West front of the 12th century, Leominster, Herefordshire.

81   Richly decorated 12th century doorway, Kilpeck, Herefordshire.

82   West tower with octagonal buttresses, Amestrey, Herefordshire.

83   Brick and tufa, Eastham, Worcestershire.

84   Sandstone at its reddest, the Perpendicular tower at Martley, Worcestershire.

85   Another red sandstone Perpendicular tower, Waverton, Cheshire.

86   Red sandstone and lias, Southam, Warwickshire.

87   The Perpendicular tower, Brailes, Warwickshire.

88   The soaring octagonal spire, Clifton Campville, Staffordshire.

89 Manor house and church, Wickhamford, Worcestershire.

90 Remote country church, a mixture of many periods, Hawkesbury, Gloucestershire.

91 Late Perpendicular timber-framed tower, Upleadon, Gloucestershire.

92   Late mediaeval oolite tower without pinnacles, Batcombe, Somerset.

93 'The Cathedral of the Forest', Newland, Gloucestershire.

94 Late 15th century oolite tower. Bruton, Somerset.

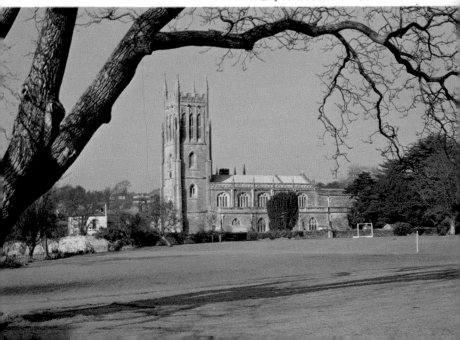

95 Cotswold church rebuilt in early 16th century, Rendcomb, Gloucestershire.

96 Blue and brown lias tower, North Petherton, Somerset.

97 Norman church, Winterborne Tomson, Dorset. Restored in memory of Thomas Hardy.

98 Perpendicular village church, Loders, Dorset.

99   Typical Devon tower with projecting stair-turret, Talaton, Devon.

100 Richly decorated red sandstone church of Perpendicular style, Cullompton, Devon.

101   Octagonal top of the late Norman tower, Colyton, Devon.

102 Country town church with transeptal towers like Exeter cathedral, Ottery St. Mary, Devon.

103 Village church of a plainer style in the same area, Branscombe, Devon.

104   Variegated serpentine stonework in the tower at Landewednack,
Cornwall.

105   Altarnun, Cornwall. Its central position is typical of the mediaeval village.

DESCRIPTION OF PLATES

4 COMMUTER COUNTRY

1 IGHTHAM, Kent. This simple Kentish tower with plain battlements and built of brown sandstone illustrates the warmth of colour to be found in the greensand country immediately south of the North Downs. The bricks used on the buttresses and on the tower itself provide a contrast of tone.

The church has fine open timber roofs of the 15th century, the nave roof being of the wagon type. It is noted for its monuments, which include one *c.* 1374 to Sir Thomas Cawne, builder of Ightham Mote manor house nearby.

2 SEAL, Kent. One of the finest of the 80 or so Kentish Perpendicular towers, normally battlemented with projecting and generally octagonal stair-turrets but usually without pinnacles. As with nearly all these towers, it is situated at the west end. Less than five miles away from Ightham and built in the 1520s of a light-toned, greenish sandstone, this sophisticated tower contrasts strikingly with the plainer one at Ightham and demonstrates the variety of colour in this area.

Among the monuments is an admirable brass, dating from 1395, of Sir William de Bryene, Lord of Kemsing and Seal.

3 WESTERHAM, Kent. Fine example of the parallel three-gable arrangement for roofing nave, aisles and chancel, common to Kent and Cornwall. Although restored, one can compare the reticulated tracery of the aisle windows with the Perpendicular tracery of the chancel window.

The church has the unique feature of a royal arms of Edward VI, the only one in the country and the oldest, except for one of Henry VIII at Rushbrooke in Suffolk.

4 AMBERLEY, Sussex. The 'catslide' method of roofing aisles, common in Sussex. The roof is brought down in one long sweep from the ridge to a few feet above the ground.

The south aisle of Amberley church was added by Bishop Ralph

Neville in 1230. He was also responsible for enlarging the chancel, doubtless to provide more space for celebrating High Mass (and to carry out ordinations) in order to cater for the many attendants he would have had with him in his position as Chancellor of the Realm.

The bishops of Selsey, and later Chichester, used adjoining Amberley Castle as a residence until the 16th century.

5 CLIMPING, Sussex. A singularly complete and well-preserved Sussex example of Early English village church architecture, almost certainly due to John de Climping who was vicar here for over 30 years, from 1220 until he became Bishop of Chichester. All the windows are lancets and their austerity contrasts with the rich exuberance of late Norman decoration on the west door and window of the tower, built of Caen stone, and the only part of the church which is earlier.

The good proportions and purity of the design give rise to the Sussex saying – 'Bosham for antiquity; Boxgrove for beauty; Climping for perfection.'

The church contains a good pre-Reformation pulpit – a rarity in Sussex – and a 13th-century Crusaders' chest, placed in churches to conform with an edict of Pope Innocent III aimed at providing funds for poor knights to go on Crusade. In the south transept a window commemorates St Wilfrid who evangelized Sussex.

6 WEST HOATHLY, Sussex. The characteristic splay-footed shingled timber spire of the south-east. The shingles, probably cedar, have weathered to a delightful silvery hue. Tower is built of Wealden sandstone. The nave and chancel are Norman.

7 PYRFORD, Surrey. St Nicholas, Pyrford, is a Surrey example of the Norman village church, largely unaltered structurally since it was built. The massive Norman walls are of a dark, flinty conglomerate or 'pudding-stone' with dressings of chalkstone. The lack of foundations has necessitated much buttressing.

The church is built on a bluff, overlooking water-meadows and the circular churchyard may well have been a pre-Christian sacred place.

8 DIDLING, Sussex. A perfect example of the unaffected charm of the Sussex hamlet church. The setting and mediaeval furnishings help to enhance this small, single-celled church.

9 HARMONDSWORTH, Middlesex. The flint and brick battlemented tower is crowned by the distinctive Middlesex 18th-century cupola.

Harmondsworth has one of the best Norman doorways in Middlesex. It also possesses a first edition of the Authorized Version of the Bible, while close to the church is a tithe barn in excellent condition, measuring 190 by 36 feet with a first-rate kingpost roof continuing over the aisles on each side. This barn is one of the largest in England.

10 MARGARETTING, Essex. One of the finest of the Essex timber towers, the rustic sturdiness acting as a counterpoint to the refined sophistication of the brick towers. The timber towers rise straight from the ground independently of the nave and, at Margaretting, the tower stands on 10 posts with strengthening as required. Vertical weatherboarding is used to cover the lower stage and shingles to cover the bell stage and spire.

The north porch is also a notable timber structure and contemporary with the 15th-century tower.

11 INGATESTONE, Essex. This tower is generally regarded as the outstanding mediaeval brick tower of Essex. Stepped battlements, a corbel frieze, a diaper pattern on the surface and a gentle taper towards the top all contribute towards producing an effect of great richness. Over 500,000 locally made bricks went into the building of this tower at the end of the 15th century.

Ingatestone Church, which is dedicated to St Edmund, the martyred king, and St Mary, has a south chapel also made of brick.

12 SANDON, Essex. Brick porches are another Essex pleasure. That at Sandon, with its stepped battlements, trefoiled corbel frieze, diaper work and diagonal buttresses, is especially notable for its accomplished brickwork, which the church probably owes to the patronage of Cardinal Wolsey. The tower also is of diapered brick and has a corbel frieze, but the battlements are straight; a boldly projecting octagonal stairturret – battlemented like the tower – rises from the north-east corner.

The church possesses a 15th century pulpit complete with stem.

5 SOUTHERN CHALK

13 HEMEL HEMPSTEAD, Hertfordshire. Hemel Hempstead is basically a Norman church with the uncommon feature of rib-vaulting in the chancel. Its lead-sheathed timber spire soars to a height of nearly 200 feet.

14 ALDENHAM, Hertfordshire. More common than lead for sheathing spires, and almost certainly cheaper, are oak shingles. They can last up to 100 years and are a suitable accompaniment to the timber spire. Aldenham uses this material on a spirelet.

The church is characteristically Hertfordshire in the use of flint and in the battlemented tower and projecting stair-turret. Although earlier styles are represented, the church is mainly Perpendicular and has a good flat timber roof of this period.

15 FELMERSHAM, Bedfordshire. The Early English style at its best in a parish church. Although the pitch of the roof has been flattened, the parapet battlemented, and there is Perpendicular tracery in the top central window of the west front, it is an Early English composition of singular beauty. This has three stages, the lowest consisting of a deeply moulded central doorway with slender shafts and flanked on each side by blank arches with plate tracery. Above this is an especially lovely arcade of seven arches decorated with dog-tooth in the mouldings, each arch supported on four detached shafts. The top stage has a wide segmental arch with pointed arches on each side.

The interior, despite later windows and some zealous restoration, preserves the same noble quality leading the eye to the stately crossing, not overshadowed as is so often the case, by the central tower. There is a 15th-century rood-screen of three bays, which unfortunately lost its loft in the restoration and, behind this, a long chancel with lancet windows. The nave has four bays divided by round and octagonal piers which alternate lengthwise and across. In the chancel is a double piscina.

16 SHELTON, Bedfordshire. A delightful mixture of seemingly haphazard alterations and sensitively restored.

17 COMPTON BEAUCHAMP, Berkshire. In contrast to the grey Totternhoe stone of Shelton, Compton Beauchamp's chalkstone is of almost dazzling whiteness and this is the dominant effect given by the exterior of this small Berkshire church, which lies next to Compton House.

Modern furnishings, which include a rood, enhance the interior, and murals, painted *c.* 1900, enliven the chancel. There are also good fragments of old glass.

18 IVINGHOE, Buckinghamshire. An impressive, battlemented church showing all the Gothic styles. It is cruciform in shape with a striking central tower crowned by a lead spike. The octagonal piers of the nave arcade, and the west doorway are decorated with stiff-leaf capitals (see Chapter 5).

The roofs, which include a panelled and decorated canopy of honour above where the rood used to exist, are adorned with figures of angels and apostles and belong to the Perpendicular period.

19 EDLESBOROUGH, Buckinghamshire. Less than five miles from Ivinghoe Church, Edlesborough, on its dominant hilltop site, has a completely different aspect from the outside. The tower is a western one, and has no spire.

The interior has similar features, with a 13th-century nave, also with octagonal piers.

Perhaps the most interesting feature is the east window with geometrical tracery which was installed when the chancel was rebuilt early in the Decorated period. This and much else has suffered from 19th-century ardour, but Edlesborough still retains its fine 15th-century roofs and notable furnishings, which include a pulpit with a most uncommon and lavish canopy in four tiers. A screen, still with the coving on the east side, and stalls with misericords depicting among other items an owl, a mermaid and a bat are also preserved.

20 MINSTER LOVELL, Oxfordshire. This church, in the Windrush Valley, is one of seven dedicated to St Kenelm which lie on the pilgrim roads to Winchcombe, Gloucestershire, where this young Mercian prince, who was murdered in the Clent Hills of Worcestershire, was buried. A remarkably complete church of the Perpendicular period and greatly enhanced by the roofing tiles, it was built by the seventh Baron Lovell in the middle of the 15th century when Oxfordshire was in the diocese of Lincoln. (It is thought that one of the carved heads may represent a former bishop of Lincoln.)

The church is notable for the vaulting under the battlemented central tower and for the arrangement of clustered piers which support it where nave, chancel and transepts meet. One can see on the piers the marks cut by the masons to check their rate of building. The font, in an unusual position in the middle of the nave, and most of the nave seating dates from the time when the church was built. There are also fragments of mediaeval glass. The central position of the tower is unusual for so late a date in a village church.

A fine alabaster altar-tomb to the builder of the church stands at the entrance to the south transept. The Lovell line died out when the last member who, according to a legend which has persisted, was accidentally buried alive in a chest in the manor-house.

21 HAMPTON POYLE, Oxfordshire. Another church situated next door to the manor-house. The grotesque capitals carved in the shape of human busts with arms interlinked are a purely local speciality.

The chancel is a good example of late 13th-century work.

22 ROTHERFIELD GREYS, Oxfordshire. In a county noted for its fine monuments (see Chapter 5), this magnificent Elizabethan memorial to the Knollys family is described by John Piper as 'one of the richest works of art for miles around'. The elephant is one of its many enjoyable features.

23 LINGFIELD, Surrey. The coloured feet are those of the effigy of the first Lord Cobham, one of the original Knights of the Garter, so being part of the earlier church before a later Lord Cobham rebuilt it as a college in the first half of the 15th century.

The Moor's-head helm at the head and this Saracen, and other strange adornments greatly add to the enjoyment of the Cobham tombs, which are the most prominent of the mediaeval monuments and fittings in Surrey's best Perpendicular church. Nairn has described the Saracen as 'part of the perennial caricaturing impulse of folk art'.

24 STANTON HARCOURT, Oxfordshire. A dignified church, as befitted the important Harcourt family who lived in the manor house next door and gave their name to the village.

The plain battlemented, unbuttressed tower is typical of many Oxfordshire towers. The blank wall space of the nave contrasts with the large window area of the south chapel, which is an elegant piece of Perpendicular work with an elaborate parapet pierced with quatrefoil circles. The woodwork inside the church includes a painted screen and a mediaeval roof. There is also some 14th-century glass.

25 STANTON HARCOURT, Oxfordshire. Among the many family memorials to the Harcourt family, this fine baroque memorial of the 17th century is the best and is a fine example of the many outstanding monuments for which Oxfordshire is noted.

26 GREAT CHALFIELD, Wiltshire. This church is intimately linked with the beautiful stone manor house, both having been built by Thomas Tropenell, a clothier, in the 15th century and both reached through the same gatehouse.

The church, has a separate Tropenell Chapel, built about 1480, which is its chief attraction; it has also both a stone and a wooden screen, and a three-decker pulpit.

Stone bellcotes, in this case with a crocketed spirelet, are a local feature in north-west Wiltshire.

27 PETERSFIELD, Hampshire. St Peter's Church has given its name to what was probably a Norman new town which sprung up around it. Although changed by a Victorian restoration of 1873–74, there is much original Norman work, dating from two phases of building, one at the beginning and the other towards the end of the 12th century. The original foundation seems to have been due to Bishop Walkelyn of Winchester, which is supported by the stylistic similarity between this church, nearby All Saints, East Meon, and the crypt, transepts and crossing of Winchester Cathedral.

This church is an impressive reminder of the wealth of Norman work in Hampshire and especially the chancel screen, at one time part of a central tower which may never have been completed. What one sees is, in fact, the inner eastern wall of this tower which was later abandoned for reasons unknown in favour of a west tower. There is rich shafting and ornamentation in the middle stage, also chevron and billet (short raised rectangles) decoration on the mouldings of the large lower arch. During restoration, the latter was braced with a plain stone arch which, being sensitively carried out, does not mar the effect.

28 BREAMORE, Hampshire. This major Saxon church lies near where, according to legend, the Saxons slew 5,000 British in battle in 519. Most of the walls and the south transept, built *c.* 1000, still remain.

It represents an early attempt towards a cruciform building but the south transept, which is little more than a chapel, is much lower and narrower than the nave and chancel, creating an unbalanced effect.

There are seven Saxon windows in various parts of the church. They are double-splayed, a mark of Saxon construction, the actual aperture for light being placed in the middle of the wall and then splayed both outwards and inwards. Some of the windows have been altered later.

A special feature is the Saxon lettering incised on the narrow arch leading to the south transept: HER SWUTELATH SEO GECWY-DRAEDNES THE – 'God's promise is revealed here.'

In the south porch, which covers the 12th-century doorway and which was erected partly in the 12th and partly in the 15th century, there is a Saxon rood, which once contained figures of the Virgin Mary and St John. The upper part of the porch retains wall-paintings and the piscina belonging to an altar, so that it seems probable that this part was built to do honour to and preserve the rood.

29 EAST WELLOW, Hampshire. A largely unspoilt 13th-century church with extensive traces of contemporary wall-paintings, including St Christopher carrying the infant Christ in his arms, rather than on his shoulder. The interior has good wooden pillars, timbered roofs, a panelled chancel and Jacobean pulpit.

Florence Nighingale spent much time at Embley Park nearby. When she died at the age of 90, she preferred a simple burial in the churchyard of East Wellow rather than a more elaborate resting-place, and a simple gravestone carved only with her initials and the years of her birth and death marks the spot.

30 BISHAM, Berkshire. This church, which has suffered much from restoration, shows how important the setting can be, for the charm of some of Berkshire's best riverside scenery is reflected in the building which lies so close to the Thames. The alabaster Hoby monuments are justifiably famous. They include a tomb-chest upon which Sir Philip and his half-brother, Sir Thomas, lie comfortably, a kneeling figure of Sir Thomas's widow, Lady Elizabeth with her children, under a canopy supported by columns, and an obelisk with four swans at the foot and a heart on top, commemorating Lady Margaret Hoby. The estate of Bisham Abbey, once an Augustinian priory and, for a short time before the Dissolution, a Benedictine abbey, was granted by Queen Mary I to the Hoby family.

6 ENGLISH LOWLANDS

31 HASLINGFIELD, Cambridgeshire. All Saints, Haslingfield has a typical Cambridgeshire tower with spike and twin-light bell-openings and transoms. The polygonal turret pinnacles, battlemented like the tower, are undoubtedly derived from Ely Cathedral. The clerestory windows and tower are Perpendicular. The clerestory windows are placed over the spandrels (triangular surfaces between arches) and not over the points of the arches. Most of the rest of the fabric is early 14th century and the walls are ashlar-faced. The unusual lead roof of the south porch dates from 1746.

32, 33 LAVENHAM, Suffolk/LONG MELFORD, Suffolk. These are among the stateliest of England's churches and, as described in the text, bear eloquent testimony to the wealth and sophistication born of wool prosperity.

34 SOUTH PICKENHAM, Norfolk. One of Norfolk's many round towers, it is situated as most of them are near a river or not far from the sea – here the River Wissey. The tower received its octagonal top later.

A faded 14th-century St Christopher can be seen on the south wall. In the 15th century the popular belief was that whoever beheld the figure of St Christopher would, for that day, be protected from evil and fatal sickness, so giving time for repentance.

35 THURTON, Norfolk. The well-trimmed thatch, a common roofing material in Norfolk, of St Ethelbert, Thurton, covers both nave and chancel (early 14th century) under one continuous roof. The late Perpendicular square turret of knapped flints and brick is an unusual structure for housing the bells.

This little church, set on an elevated site near the road from Norwich to Lowestoft, has a richly decorated Norman south door.

36 SOUTHWOLD, Suffolk. Dedicated to St Edmund, King and Martyr, this is one of the grand East Anglian churches, completely rebuilt in the 15th century after the old church had been destroyed by fire. It stretches in one long, unbroken line nearly 150 feet and has a tower 100 feet high.

Flushwork is used lavishly in panels on the buttresses of the tower and in the form of lozenge decoration on the parapet. A pleasing chequerboard design is applied to the west face and also on the sides of the magnificent south porch, which is also decorated with flushwork panelling. This latter treatment is also used round the base of the church below the windows.

The serried line of clerestory and the large aisle windows below give the open, glasshouse effect so sought after by 15th-century masons, and produces a beautifully light interior, while the wooden fittings, which include excellent stalls, pulpit and painted screen stretching right across nave and aisles, are mainly of the same date as the fabric of the building. The slender nave piers complete the stately effect without ostentation. 'Southwold Jack', the clock jack on the north side of the tower arch, strikes the bell with an axe to mark the beginning of services, and is a perfect representation of a man-at-arms at the end of the 15th century, complete with blood-flecked eyes and unshaven chin.

In common with East Anglian practice, there are no pinnacles or battlements to crown the tower.

37 WEST WALTON, Norfolk. West Walton, together with Walsoken and Walpole St Peter form a trio of magnificent churches where almost every mediaeval style can be studied within a very small area.

A board hanging in the south aisle of West Walton records three great floods which submerged all this marshland area in 1613, 1614 and in 1671.

West Walton is one of the finest Early English parish churches in England and dates from the mid-13th century. The detached tower has open arches on all four sides at the base and beautiful tapering polygonal buttresses.

38 WALPOLE ST PETER, Norfolk. Although only a village church, Walpole St Peter is over 160 feet long. It is largely built of limestone, not flint. All but the tower was destroyed in a great flood in 1337, and it was rebuilt with money generated from a change-over of agriculture from crops to sheep-farming. In a passage under the high altar, there is a carving of a sheep's head. This passage, locally called 'The Bolt Hole', was probably part of a processional way, constructed in this manner because of insufficient consecrated ground east of the church. The effect of this is to raise the altar nine steps above the rest of the chancel, creating a focal point which carries the eye up to the most sacred part of the building. The chancel is further enhanced by stone canopies over the stalls – a most unusual feature.

The south porch, which contains many fine bosses, is a further asset to a church which can justifiably claim to be one of the finest village churches in England.

39 SWANTON MORLEY, Norfolk. All Saints, Swanton Morley, is especially interesting because it is very early but developed Perpendicular, having been built at the end of the 14th century.

The exceptionally tall bell-openings in the tower and the clerestory window at the east end of the nave recall Yorkshire features, although there seems to be no connection. The aisles extend to the west end of the tower and so embrace it. Flushwork is used in a panelled frieze along the west side of the church and above this a frieze of quatrefoils. There is also much enjoyable window tracery.

40 ATTLEBOROUGH, Norfolk. Perhaps nowhere else in England is the importance of the rood in mediaeval churches so well demonstrated. Although the rood is no longer there, the loft which remains at Attleborough is the finest in England. The whole of the parapet on the west side is completely preserved, displaying along the front the heraldic arms of the 24 episcopal sees then existing which were painted after the Reformation. The loft, apart from acting in many cases as a base for the rood, enabling people to clean and light it, also provided accommodation for the choir and instrumentalists.

The painting behind, which provided a background to the rood, has been carefully restored. It shows, among other figures, Moses and David.

St Mary has lost its Norman chancel and apse, also chancel chapels, so that the tower, of which the base is also Norman, is no longer a crossing tower.

There is much Decorated tracery, known as the four-petalled flower, especially noteworthy in the five-light west window.

41 CAWSTON, Norfolk. St Agnes, Cawston is another of the great Norfolk churches. At the beginning of the 15th century, it was largely – but not completely – rebuilt in the Perpendicular style (the chancel and south transept are Decorated).

The hammer-beam roof is generally regarded as one of the finest in East Anglia. Angels with outspread wings are placed along the wall as well as on the hammer-beams themselves and there are numerous bosses. A few traces of wall-painting can be seen, perhaps like Attleborough, a background to the rood.

The tall, gaunt tower is devoid of battlements, pinnacles or even a parapet, but has a decorated base course.

42 TATTERSHALL, Lincolnshire. Built by Lord Ralph Cromwell in the mid-15th century, his badge, a purse, is very conspicuous. Lord Ralph was Treasurer during the reign of Henry VI. This collegiate church, constructed of oolite, is a sumptuous monument to the power of this man, who lived in the adjoining castle, but is strangely devoid of furnishings. This, the lack of cusping in the window tracery, and the absence of the contemporary glass, except for a varied assortment in the east window, gives a bare look to the interior and unduly accentuates the glasshouse effect.

A curiosity is the existence of two pulpits, both of wood, one of which is in the nave and the other in the chancel.

43 GEDNEY, Lincolnshire. This has a fine clerestory, a dominant exterior feature which runs above a Decorated aisle. The church has Early English features, too, for the lower part of the tower is 13th century; it blends well with the tall Perpendicular top stage, which is only marred by an inadequate lead spike instead of the intended spire.

This handsome, ashlar-faced building was under Crowland Abbey, the most important Benedictine house of Lincolnshire, which no doubt accounts for its richness. The two-storied south porch contains a fine, richly decorated door and there is much variety in the window tracery.

44 STOW, Lincolnshire. St Mary, Stow, has the mightiest Saxon chancel arch in the country, appropriate to a church which, there is reason to believe, was as large in Saxon times as it is today.

7 EASTERN MIDLANDS

45 SPALDWICK, Huntingdonshire. St James, Spaldwick, possesses one of the best broach spires of Huntingdonshire. The broach, a triangular mass of masonry, links the square tower to the octagonal spire.

Broach spires are usually sparing of ornament, this being largely restricted to the top of the tower and the spire-lights (there are three tiers at Spaldwick) and their gables. The beauty of these spires depends on the proportion of and the relation of the angle of the broach to the spire. Spaldwick has bold carved projections at the top of the broaches, like gargoyles.

St James has all mediaeval styles: a Norman north door, the chancel Early English with interesting late Geometrical tracery, the 150-foot tower and south nave arcade Decorated, and the south aisle and chapel Perpendicular.

46 EMPINGHAM, Rutland. A noble, mainly 13th-century church with a 14th-century battlemented tower which is richly and variously decorated. The crocketed stone spire is short in relation to the tower but this is characteristic of this spire county.

47 TICKENCOTE, Rutland. St Peter's is noted for its prodigious chancel arch, in which the builder's aspirations appear to have exceeded his skill, for it is noticeably depressed in the centre. The decoration includes zigzag, beakhead and other motifs and there are five richly shafted orders.

The building has suffered much from late 18th-century attempts to improve on the original, but the form of vaulting in the chancel pre-dates even one of the earliest uses of it in Canterbury Cathedral and the east end is a striking example of Norman work.

48 KIRBY BELLARS, Leicestershire. Also dedicated to St Peter, it is built of an attractive brown ironstone combined with limestone.

Collegiate from 1315, it became a house of Augustinian Canons as from 1359.

The west tower is completed with a richly decorated ashlar-faced spire with very small broaches. The nave arcade is 13th century, but otherwise it is mainly Decorated with a Perpendicular clerestory.

49 KETTON, Rutland. Although in the midst of a fine stone district, this church is built of Barnack material. It was only later that Ketton oolite came into fashion. Ketton spire became the prototype most admired by the Victorians and one can see 19th-century 'Kettons' all over the country. The tower is 13th century and a good example of Early English work. The west front is an especially interesting instance of the transition from Norman to Early English. The rest of the church is mainly 13th century.

50 BRIXWORTH, Northamptonshire. The south door is one of the few post-Saxon features in this major pre-Conquest building. It is, in fact, the only remaining Norman work, although there was a porch which was dismantled during the 19th century. The door has roll-mouldings and simple shafts. In the beautiful warm ironstone above, one can see Roman bricks roughly constructed into arches.

51 NORTHAMPTON. Two Crusades started from Northampton, one in 1239 and the other in 1270 and Richard Cœur de Lion kept Easter here at the end of the 12th century after his return from captivity. The first Norman Earl of Northampton, who went on the earlier Crusade, founded, at the beginning of the 12th century, this church of the Holy Sepulchre, no doubt as a thank-offering for his safe return.

It is one of four with round naves to survive in England (there are the remains of a fifth in Ludlow Castle, Shropshire) and one of only two which have always been parish churches (the other is at Cambridge, also dedicated to the Holy Sepulchre). They were built in this form in imitation of the rotunda of the church of the Holy Sepulchre at Jerusalem.

The church at Northampton originally consisted of the round nave and a long, straight chancel, but the nave was later heightened, although the fine round columns remain, and the chancel widened with aisles. An amusing row of corbels which at one time supported a roof remain in the chancel. They consist of people playing musical instruments.

Most of the part illustrated in the plate, including the apse, is a Victorian reconstruction of the 1860s, but it also shows the colour of the stone and the fine 14th-century tower and spire.

52 TEVERSAL, Nottinghamshire. St Catherine, Teversal, is near the industrial coal-mining area of the Notts/Derby border. It is noted for its post-Reformation furnishings which include a full set of box-pews in the nave and a squire's pew complete with barley-sugar columns.

53 CUCKNEY, Nottinghamshire. Like Teversal, Cuckney lies near the Nottinghamshire/Derbyshire coal mines, but it is also on the edge of the Dukeries, an area of large private estates. The church dates from the early part of the mediaeval period and is distinctive because of its long nave and varied piers.

54 CARLTON-IN-LINDRICK, Nottinghamshire. This is a notable Nottinghamshire Norman church with a striking west door. The tower is earlier, although crowned by 15th-century battlements and numerous rather slender pinnacles. It was also buttressed at that time.

55 WHISTON, Northamptonshire. The church is virtually unaltered since it was built by Anthony Catesby in the early part of the 16th century and is, therefore, a singularly complete church of this period. The orange lias and grey oolite which were used for constructing the fine tower provide a rare colour contrast. The absence of a chancel arch gives a spacious effect to the rectangular interior, but the window tracery, although positive, is somewhat repetitive.

56 BAKEWELL, Derbyshire. All Saints, Bakewell, is clearly a town church, predominant as it should be and presenting a typical Derbyshire profile – 'rather low and broad, embattled, and with a tower and spire' – to quote Pevsner. This is a carboniferous limestone region, but the churches tend to be of a dark pinkish-grey colour.

The Victorians were active in this part of England, as in so many other areas, and the nave and octagonal upper stage of the tower were among the parts rebuilt in the 19th century. All Saints was collegiate and was handed over by King John to Lichfield Cathedral. There is Norman and later work of all mediaeval styles in the church. The monuments include a small 14th-century upright one to Sir Godfrey Foljambe and his wife, one of the very few cases of mediaeval effigies being in an upright and not recumbent position.

57 BONSALL, Derbyshire. The income from the export of local lead in mediaeval times may have been responsible for the elegant spire of St James, with its two ornamental bands and ashlar finish. The building has the characteristic low battlemented profile and pinkish-grey stone of Derbyshire.

58 WIRKSWORTH, Derbyshire. Wirksworth has many things in common with Bakewell. It belonged to Lichfield Cathedral; it is in the centre of a town; it has been much Victorianized and is of a similar stone. Like Bonsall, it is also in the lead-mining district and there is an appealing stone carving of a miner with his pick.

Over 150 feet long and set in an ample churchyard, St Mary's is an impressive building, the effect perhaps slightly diminished by the rather inadequate Hertfordshire spike, so far from home.

59 TIDESWELL, Derbyshire. Hidden away in a remote moorland district, this is among the grandest of the Derbyshire churches and the least restored, and deserves its title of 'Cathedral of the Peak'. It has a superb chancel, the tall and broad windows of which have square heads.

Other assets are the consistency of its notable 14th-century architecture and its highly individual, if perhaps rather heavy, Perpendicular tower with eight pinnacles, the corner ones having been developed into polygonal turrets. In addition, Tideswell is rich in pre-Reformation monuments and possesses a stone screen behind the altar.

8 THE NORTHERN MARCHES AND YORKSHIRE

60 ISEL, Cumberland. This Norman building is set beside the River Derwent, not far from Isel Hall. It seems probable that preaching started here at the point where a forest track crossed the river and that a cross, either wooden or stone, was erected to mark the spot; later, a simple shelter for worship may have been constructed which developed gradually into the present church.

The main feature, internally is the beautiful chancel arch, *c.* 1130. In the jamb of a chancel window are three sundials for determining the hours of Mass and the church possesses three pre-Conquest sculptured stones, including one with a rare three-legged symbol called the 'triskele' (three legs of Man), discovered when a bridge nearby was rebuilt in 1812.

61 WHITBY, North Riding, Yorkshire. The gruff exterior, so suited to the windy, clifftop site belies the 18th-century charm of the interior. The glorious hugger-mugger of box-pews, galleries and the famous Cholmley squire's pew with its barley-sugar columns, all focus on the high pulpit and reading-desk.

At the Synod of Whitby, held in 663 at the original abbey next door under the supervision of the Abbess Hilda, far-reaching decisions were taken to link the English Church with the Roman rather than the Celtic ritual.

62 SEAMER, North Riding, Yorkshire. Seamer, three miles south-west of Scarborough, is mainly Norman, as exemplified by the tower, although the latter was rebuilt in 1840. The church is battlemented and unexpectedly long with a wide nave. It has a fine, Jacobean pulpit.

There is a sanctus bellcote on the east gable of the nave.

63 HEMINGBROUGH, East Riding, Yorkshire. The Decorated period was a great age for building parish churches in the East Riding, though this is not reflected at Hemingbrough, for St Mary's church is mainly Early English and Perpendicular. Its fine 15th-century spire (a late date for spires), rises twice as high as the tower.

The church was under Durham Monastery and became collegiate at the beginning of the 15th century. The fine stalls with poppy-heads and good bench-ends mainly decorated with tracery but with a jester as well, may be due to this. The misericord with leaf trail in the south-west stall may be the earliest in England, c. 1200. The lofty transepts have large Perpendicular windows and the south aisle is Tudor.

Hemingbrough lies in a magnesian limestone region and St Mary's is built of a very white variety quarried at Tadcaster.

64 BIRKIN, West Riding, Yorkshire. The village church at Birkin is one of the finest Norman places of worship in Yorkshire. The only later additions are the Decorated south aisle and tracery in the east window, and the Perpendicular top to the tower. The latter is tall and unbuttressed.

The church is built of ashlar, while windows and arches are shafted and decorated with Norman motifs. The south doorway is especially fine and the original corbel-tables remain in nave, chancel and apse. This church, too, is built of the white magnesian limestone quarried at Tadcaster.

65 WEST TANFIELD, North Riding, Yorkshire. Church and castle gatehouse make an inseparable group above the bank of the River Ure. Distance lends some enchantment to the mainly 15th-century church, for it was drastically restored in the 19th century. A strange recess in the north chapel may have been connected with a chantry chapel for the Marmion family, who lived in the castle and who are commemorated by memorials, including a superb alabaster tomb still retaining its original wrought-iron hearse with scones for candles.

66 ESCOMB, Durham. A moving reminder of what northern churches were like in the days when Bede was alive. Escomb church was largely built of squared stone from the Roman camp of Vinovia, two miles to the north. In the north wall, there is even a stone marked LEG VI, the sign of the Roman 6th Legion which replaced the 9th at York about 122 and may have had a detachment at Vinovia. Towards the top of the wall the stones are smaller and it would seem that the supply from the camp ran out.

As with Bradford-on-Avon in Wiltshire and Odda's chapel at Deerhurst in Gloucestershire, we owe it to the Victorians that these early places of worship were discovered and restored.

67 STAINDROP, Durham. The few churches in England dedicated to St Gregory are all of Saxon foundation, and Staindrop, which was at one time so dedicated, is no exception. It has been confirmed that a Saxon church was built on this site as early as the 8th century.

The building, now dedicated to St Mary, has work of all mediaeval periods with refreshingly little from the 19th century. The lords of Raby Castle nearby appear to have looked after it well.

There are some fine monuments, including one in alabaster dated *c.* 1425 to the Earl of Westmorland and his two wives. It was he who founded a college for priests and laymen here in 1422.

The tower, enclosed by the aisles, is unbuttressed and the early 15th-century top stage is corbelled out to produce a wider top, normally against the rules of good tower composition, but none the less a success and giving a particularly northern look to the tower, probably copied from castles.

The chancel has fine sedilia.

68 CORBRIDGE, Northumberland. Corbridge, like Escomb, used Roman material for the building of its church. It came from the Roman town of Corstopitum, half a mile to the west, and included a complete gateway which was moved from the town to provide an arch between the tower and nave. The lower parts of the tower date from the 8th century, when the church was a monastery. In 786 Aldulf was consecrated as Bishop of Mayo 'in the monastery which is called Corabridge'.

Later construction is mainly of the 13th century, but the south doorway inside the 19th-century porch is Norman. The chancel, in particular, is excellent Early English work with a striking group of stepped lancets at the east end.

The turbulence of the north in mediaeval times is graphically emphasized by the Vicar's Pele tower built about 1300 of mainly Roman stones, in the churchyard to the south-east. These towers were fortified residences for the incumbent. During Scottish raids or other troubles, the cattle could be driven into the basement, the middle floor used as living quarters and the upper part for sleeping accommodation or defence.

69 HALTWHISTLE, Northumberland. One of the best examples of Northumbrian Early English, a period strongly represented in the county. The church of the Holy Cross has no tower, only a gable. This, however, does not detract from the singularly complete and well-preserved 13th-century building with lancets in all walls, including those of the clerestories. There are no less than 11 in the chancel, including three at the east end which are stepped.

70 LANERCOST, Cumberland. Here again, Roman material is re-used in a later building. This priory of Augustinian Canons, founded in the 1160s, was built from materials used in the Roman wall. It was also on the route of the warring English and Scottish armies, and suffered from Scottish raids.

Although dissolved in Henry VIII's reign, what remains is still impressive. The nave, in red and grey sandstone, has survived as the parish church, and the choir, although open to the sky, still rises to roof level. The façade is a beautiful piece of Early English work with a richly moulded doorway, surmounted by a trefoiled arcade and, above that, three stepped lancets with an original statue of St Mary Magdalene in a niche in the gable.

71 GRASMERE, Westmorland. A church indissolubly linked with the poet, Wordsworth, who is buried in the churchyard together with members of his family. The dedication is to St Oswald, the Christian Northumbrian king who was killed in battle with Penda, the Mercian king.

The great feature of the church is the ingenious roof, constructed in the 17th century, to support which a second line of arches had to be built above the 16th-century nave, thus creating a two-storied arcade. The font is believed to have come from Furness Abbey.

72 BEETHAM, Westmorland. This low, partly battlemented church is half Norman and half Perpendicular. The lower stage of the tower is 12th and the corbelled-out upper stage (cf. Staindrop) is 16th century, while the south arcade of the nave is 12th and the north 15th century. Fragments of 15th-century stained glass remain in the south chapel and the west window of the tower.

73 HAWKSHEAD, Lancashire. Wordsworth's 'snow-white church upon her hill' sitting 'like a thronèd lady' is no longer as he saw it, for the white plaster has been removed and the grey Silurian stone exposed. Inside, however, the plaster remains and has been used as a surface upon which to paint texts and as a background for numerous wall-tablets. The arches, too, of the arcades and the heads of the piers have been outlined with geometrically patterned yellow and black margins.

St Michael's Church is basically late 15th or early 16th century to which in 1578, Archbishop Sandys added a north aisle. The construction is simple and the nave piers have neither capitals nor bases, but it is appropriate for this beautifully sited church, which harmonizes with some of the grandest scenery in England.

74 CARTMEL, Lancashire. Lancashire's greatest mediaeval church was founded not long after Lanercost, also as a priory for Augustinian Canons, but, as it was the parish church, it was spared at the Dissolution and is a rare example of a mediaeval priory church which is still complete.

It was a slow-growth building of many periods, the Norman being represented by the chancel apart from the east window and a superb south door, the Early English by the north transept, the Decorated by the south chapel with flowing tracery windows and the Perpendicular by the short nave, the enormous east window of 9 lights and the unique arrangement of the top stage of the tower being set diagonally on the part below it.

The church is of great interest, with the fine but damaged Harrington tomb of the mid-14th century, one of the best of this date in the country, and the outstanding stalls, which are of a slightly later date than the misericords. The latter include a doctor represented as an ape holding a flask (the mediaeval medical profession was regarded as artful as an ape), a double-tailed mermaid and an elephant and castle. There are small but good remains of a 14th-century Jesse window in the south chapel.

It is also a pattern-book of building materials, incorporating lime-stone and slate rubble for the walls, red sandstone and millstone grit for the piers, Caen stone for the great east window.

The reprieved priory was roofless for 80 years after the Dissolution until it was restored by a member of the Preston family, who had acquired much of the priory property.

9 WEST MIDLANDS

75 ASTBURY, Cheshire. This is a fine example of a Cheshire church, mainly Perpendicular but with older parts as well. It stands in a commanding position at the top of the small sloping funnel-shaped green, drawing the eye to the battlemented west front and the 14th-century detached tower and spire.

The battlemented south side with noticeably tall clerestory windows which add to the dignity of the building is of millstone grit, rare in Cheshire, which has weathered well and preserved the crisp tracery of the windows.

Internally, there is no chancel arch and the pink and grey arcade has no capitals so that the arches die into the piers. The wealth of woodwork includes 15th-century screen and stalls, and truly magnificent roofs, low-pitched and with camber-beams, as is usual in Cheshire, with bosses and pendants. Among post-mediaeval furnishings are an elaborate font-cover with canopy, box-pews and communion rail.

76 KINETON, Warwickshire. St Peter's is largely rebuilt, but the tower provides another colour which might be described as orange-brown – striking a vivid note in contrast with the blue lias of the cottages to the south-east.

The tower with its elaborate crown is a mixture of 13th- and 15th-century work. There is an excellent richly shafted and moulded west doorway.

77 CLEOBURY MORTIMER, Shropshire. The church lies at the east end of the town of Cleobury Mortimer. It is a satisfying building, constructed of a yellowish sandstone, in the styles of the early mediaeval era, delightfully consistent and fairly gently restored. The tower is a mixture of Norman and Early English, completed with a tall, shingled spire of south-eastern England vintage. It has a pronounced twist.

The richly shafted chancel arch is outstanding with good stiff-leaf capitals, which can also be seen on the south door, and the roofs of nave and chancel are excellent 14th-century work.

78, 79 STOKESAY, Shropshire/CROFT, Herefordshire. St John Baptist at Stokesay and St Michael's at Croft are both small and the size of the castles nearby accentuates this.

Although neither of the churches is outstanding, St John's has a very rare example of a nave built in the period of Oliver Cromwell's rule (1650s) and, to preserve the balance, a tower built a decade later when the king had been restored to his throne. The south doorway is Norman.

St Michael's has a 13th-century nave and chancel, and 18th-century box-pews and gallery, but perhaps its most attractive feature is the 17th-century bell-turret with balustrade and lead-covered ogee cap.

80 LEOMINSTER, Herefordshire. This pink sandstone church formed part of a Benedictine monastery which Henry I bestowed upon his favourite foundation, Reading Abbey, and the famous Herefordshire school of Norman sculpture may well owe its origin to this abbey.

Leominster church had three building periods – Norman, when the original nave (now the north aisle) was erected, Early English, when the parish nave was added and 14th century when a south aisle was built. All the eastern parts have disappeared and the effect, on entry, is of three naves suddenly stopping short. The west doorway, which has unusual capitals (two birds, two reapers and two writhing serpents) is a fine piece of Norman work with hints of a point in the arch as early as 1150, although this was probably for structural reasons; the south porch is Early English but reset later and given three Decorated niches which are embellished with ball-flower ornament. This favourite form of Decorated treatment is used lavishly on the south aisle windows. The west tower is 15th but the crown 19th century.

81 KILPECK, Herefordshire. St Mary and St David is one of the most sumptuously decorated Norman village churches in England and, thanks to the resistant sandstone of which it was built, it is one of the best preserved. Apart from the bellcote, there has been little later alteration. The Benedictines founded a priory at Kilpeck in 1134.

Here the Herefordshire school of sculpture is at its most exuberant, especially on the jambs of the south door, the 74 corbels of the corbel-table which runs right round the church, and on the chancel arch.

Scandinavian influence in some of the decoration is clear, the protruding jaws with long curling tongues on the pilasters of the west wall, for example, but there are other sources as well which are not so obvious. Robert Stoll, in his *Architecture and Sculpture in Early Britain*, gives a fascinating interpretation of what he calls 'the church's sculptural programme which the 12th-century Christian regarded primarily as religious instruction – a sermon preached by frieze, capital and portal –

and only secondarily as decoration.' Basically this represents the eternal struggle between the forces of evil and the forces of good, the latter symbolized by the tree of life in the tympanum of the south door and leading one towards the calm and serenity of the figures of the apostles on the chancel arch.

Among the animals carved on the corbels are a dog and donkey on the apse. In the jambs are warriors with head-dresses like Phrygian caps.

82 AYMESTREY, Herefordshire. Dedicated to St John Baptist and St Alkmund, this church of red sandstone lies in a typical, unassuming Herefordshire setting. The sturdy, battlemented west tower has diagonal buttresses and is capped by a striking weathercock. The entrance inside is tunnel-vaulted.

The interior has a notable rood-screen, the best in the county, which was installed in the 16th century. It has linenfold panelling on the dado, lierne ribs on the coving, friezes on the cornice, and cresting. There are also simpler parclose screens (separating a chapel from the rest of the church).

83 EASTHAM, Worcestershire. It displays many purely local characteristics: first, in the use of tufa stone; second in the projection of the Norman south door from the wall; third, in the sculptured, now very weathered, representation of Sagittarius and Leo on the south walls.

84 MARTLEY, Worcestershire. Martley Church, which lies in the heart of the west Worcestershire fruit-growing country, is noted for its reddest of red towers. This is 15th century, but nave and chancel are Norman and the roofs (restored) 14th century.

There is no division between nave and chancel. During restoration in 1909, many wall-paintings were uncovered, including masonry and curtain patterns with fabulous beasts in the top loops of the curtain. These are in the chancel but there are others.

85 WAVERTON, Cheshire. Like so many churches in the red sandstone country, Waverton has had to be extensively restored and the wall surface has lost its texture of old age and acquired a smooth patina. The tower is Perpendicular, but with a 19th-century pyramid roof. There is timber-framing in the chancel.

86 SOUTHAM, Warwickshire. This church has a fine broach spire, further enhanced by pinnacles on the broaches. The stone is a mixture of lias and red sandstone, ringing yet another colour change. The tower is 14th and the spire 15th century. St James has a clerestory with eight closely set windows. The nave roof is of low pitch.

87 BRAILES, Warwickshire. St George's is one of the most interesting churches in Warwickshire and its size reflects the importance of the town, which was probably at one time second only to Coventry and Warwick in the county. In the 14th century, it had a thriving water-mill and a valuable wool trade.

Hemmed in on the west by a house, it stretches unrestrictedly, towards the lower ground to the east – over 150 feet. 'The Cathedral of Feldon', as the rolling country south of the River Avon is called, is mainly a Decorated building. It has a nave over 150 feet long, and an imposing Perpendicular west tower 110 feet high. The south porch, with its openwork parapet also dates from the 15th century, but the openwork parapet on the south aisle is 14th century and so, too, is the handsome east window, a notable example of reticulated or net tracery. The 14th-century font has a deep bowl, large enough for total immersion and there is a notable 15th-century chest.

The clerestories have 12 windows on each side and the gable of the one on the north side is completed with a delightful sanctus bell-turret.

Brailes appears to have suffered during the Civil War (Edgehill is not far away), but the Commonwealth restoration is obscured by a 'doing over' in the 19th century.

88 CLIFTON CAMPVILLE, Staffordshire. What Brailes is to Warwickshire, Clifton Campville might be deemed to be to Staffordshire, although very different in appearance. It is built of a now blackened grey sandstone and has a tall spire, whereas Brailes has none. The churches are, however, similar in that they are both mainly Decorated and among the finest in their respective counties.

Clifton Campville's interior is open and light with a fine queenpost roof and has a little of most things – wall-paintings, old glass, monuments, stalls with misericords and screens.

89 WICKHAMFORD, Worcestershire. This has an enjoyable collection of box-pews, panelling in the chancel, west gallery with carvings from a London church, and 18th-century communion rail. Above the chancel arch is a beam with cresting, surmounted by a tympanum with Charles II's royal arms. These are typical post-Reformation furnishings, which have so often been frowned upon by the Victorians and swept away. There is a superb alabaster double monument of 1626 in the chancel to Sir Samuel and Sir Edwin Sandys and their wives.

10 CELT AND SAXON

90 HAWKESBURY, Gloucestershire. St Mary's Church is mainly of the 15th century, with the unusual feature of a rise of nine steps from west to east, focusing attention on the chancel.

The tower is of six stages and dates from the 14th century, except for the Perpendicular battlemented parapet with gargoyles, and the stair-turret capped by a small spire. The chancel is largely Early English but with some later windows. Hawkesbury has one of Gloucestershire's 20 mediaeval stone pulpits.

91 UPLEADON, Gloucestershire. A beautifully restored, remote rural church of a type by no means common in Gloucestershire. It is built on a mound of clay. The tall and closely set studs (upright beams) of the charming timber tower are mainly filled with brick. The fabric consists of a Norman nave, entered through a north doorway which has a tympanum carved with an Agnus Dei, and a Victorian chancel.

92, 96 BATCOMBE/NORTH PETHERTON, Somerset. The towers of Bruton, Batcombe and North Petherton are among the finest in Somerset, and so in England.

The tower of Batcombe is also built of Doulting oolite but has no pinnacles. Instead, there is a fine, pierced straight parapet with quatre-foils. The three windows in the upper stage are continued into the stage below (cf St Cuthbert's Wells, Evercreech) and thus form one complete stage above the roof-line. The west wall, built 1540–41, is decorated with stone carvings of Christ in glory, attended by three pairs of angels.

North Petherton is built of blue lias and Ham Hill stone. Many writers regard the latter as oolite, although modern geology classifies it as a lias. This, one of the most beautiful of all towers, is described in Chapter 10. It has an elaborate parapet, many pinnacles, and the upper stage has two belfry windows which have transoms, as do the windows below.

The exterior of Batcombe church is enriched with pierced parapets above the aisles, but the masons have really concentrated on the tower, and the interior, especially the chancel, is relatively small in comparison. North Petherton has mediaeval roofs and a pre-Reformation pulpit.

93 NEWLAND, Gloucestershire. 'The Cathedral of the Forest' has a fine tower, begun at the turn of the 13th/14th century and completed towards the end of the Decorated period with five pinnacles and a pierced parapet. Four of the pinnacles are fluted, but the fifth over the stair-turret is plain. The tower thus satisfies one of the criteria of good tower composition by increasing in interest towards the top.

Of the many monuments, including a number of early ones, the effigy of the Forester of Fee is of special interest because it shows the hunting costume of the mid-15th century. In the south aisle is a flat slab with the incised figure of a bowman of the early 17th century. These two and the miner mentioned in Chapter 10 provide an interesting picture of the dress and equipment of members of the community who were not usually commemorated in those times.

94 BRUTON, Somerset. St Mary's, built of Doulting stone, is a worthy example of Somerset churches at their best. The fine tower will be considered in the next description, along with two other out-standing ones. The interior is mainly of 15th-century work, but has a Georgian chancel. There are admirable mediaeval timber roofs, the nave roof-beams resting on shafts with stone niches, which are filled with Victorian statuary. The crypt below the chancel is of the early 14th century.

Bruton is battlemented, with some pinnacles, and the three windows in the upper stage, all pierced for the sound of the bells, lead the eye naturally to the top. The battlements are decorated with shields and quatrefoils, and there are many niches for statues.

The chancel, which is sensitively restored, combines harmoniously with the Perpendicular nave and provides a bright touch of colour.

95 RENDCOMB, Gloucestershire. Unlike other Cotswold churches, St Peter's has no chancel arch, but a wooden screen stretches across both nave and aisle. Characteristically, however, it was all rebuilt in the early part of the 16th century of golden-grey Cotswold ashlar stone. This was due to the wealth brought by the wool trade to Sir Edwin Tame, the son of John Tame who built Fairford in the same county.

From an earlier period comes the fine Norman tub-shaped font, very similar to the one at Hereford Cathedral, with figures of 11 apostles carved round the bowl but the twelfth, Judas, uncarved. There are many fragments of glass, contemporary with the Fairford glass but of a different style.

97 WINTERBORNE TOMSON, Dorset. This church is an endearing example of a single-celled, apsed, hamlet-type church, beautifully restored after long disuse by A. R. Powys in 1936, in memory of Thomas Hardy.

The interior has a wagon roof, a complete set of Georgian fittings and fine west gallery, which was once the front of the mediaeval rood-loft.

98 LODERS, Dorset. St Mary Magdalene is a charming, honey-coloured village church of all mediaeval periods, standing close to the manor house. The manor of Loders at one time belonged to a Normandy abbey, the monks of whom brought with them, it is alleged, the art of cider-making.

The predominantly Perpendicular architecture consists of the tower, south porch with turret-staircase leading to the upper floor, the south aisle and the two-bay nave arcade. An ogee-headed recess for an Easter Sepulchre in the chancel north wall was discovered during a restoration at the end of the 19th century. But, even more exciting was to find under the plaster on the north wall of the nave three narrow doorways, one above the other two, all connected by a spiral stairway. These were the entrances to the mediaeval pulpit and to the rood-loft, and so far as is known there is no other combination like this.

The exterior is much battlemented.

99 TALATON, Devon. This is a little-known example of a typical Devon tower with projecting stair-turret. The niches for statues at the top have most of their original figures preserved.

The nave, with only two bays, and south aisle are Perpendicular, the north aisle is 19th century.

100 CULLOMPTON, Devon. St Andrew's is one of Devonshire's grandest churches. Externally, it is all in red sandstone, except for the use of Beer chalkstone and Ham Hill lias on the tower carvings, and all in one style. Beer stone is also used for the nave arcades. It has clerestories, which is unusual for Devon. The tower and aisle are all battlemented and there is a carving of sheep shears and ships on the south aisle wall to show from where the money came.

The glory of the exterior is the 100-foot tower with stair-turret, pierced battlements, numerous pinnacles and further enrichments. The glories of the interior are the sumptuous aisle built in the 1520s by John Lane, a wealthy clothier, and the splendid coloured roof which runs from end to end. The Lane aisle has an elaborate stone fan-vault and the nave/chancel roof is of timber. In addition, there is a wooden rood-screen, also coloured, running across both nave and aisles. A surprising survival is a Golgotha, consisting of rocks, skulls and bones which formed the base of the rood itself. This can be seen at the west end of the Lane aisle.

Later wooden furnishings include 19th-century box pews, squire's pew and gallery.

101 COLYTON, Devon. Central towers, as well as clerestories, are rare in Devon but Colyton has one with an octagonal top.

The well-lit 15th-century nave has aisles almost as wide as the nave, but the upper parts were renewed in the 18th and 19th centuries and the roofs, after a fire, in 1933. The chancel is basically Norman with Perpendicular aisles. There are two stone screens to chapels, one pre-Reformation and one Jacobean.

An interesting survival is an almost complete Saxon cross dating from 900, found after the fire. The Normans took it to pieces and used it for building the tower, whence it was recovered and put together again – a clear case of Norman disrespect for anything Saxon. The shaft is decorated with scrolls and interlacings.

The material of which the church is built includes chert, a kind of brown flint with a curious, semi-transparent look. It is cut into squared blocks as large as bricks. This is a purely local material.

102 OTTERY ST MARY, Devon. Although externally not as impressive as Cullompton, this is another of Devon's major mediaeval parish churches. Apart from the earlier transeptal towers, which echo those at Exeter, and the transepts they cover, St Mary's reflects the munificence of Bishop Grandisson of Exeter, who made it collegiate in the 1330s. He rebuilt the nave, chancel, aisles and Lady Chapel, providing the chancel with an unusual form of vaulting with curved ribs, and equipping the church with a stone reredos (restored), sedilia, stalls with misericords, screens, wooden eagle lectern (early) and the rare clock in the south transept. It also has a clerestory.

Later in the 16th century, the Dorset aisle was added under Bishops Oldham and Vesey, sumptuously fan-vaulted like the Lane aisle at Cullompton. The church also has many monuments.

103 BRANSCOMBE, Devon. This is another Devonshire church which owes much to its bishops, one of whom, Bishop Branscombe, appears to have taken his name from the place. The church, once belonged to St Peter's, Exeter. All mediaeval periods are represented, starting with the Norman crossing tower – except for the top – continuing with the Early English transepts, the 14th-century chancel and ending with the Perpendicular additions of east window (replaced by Bishop Neville), and the wagon roof.

The interior has a wealth of wooden furnishings, including an 18th-century three-decker pulpit, a rarity in Devon. There are box-pews, west gallery, screen and altar-rails from varying dates.

104 LANDEWEDNACK, Cornwall. St Winwallo (one of the many unusual Cornish dedications) is the most southerly church in England. Serpentine and granite is used in its construction and serpentine is seen – black and greenish – in the tower. It is one of the chief building materials of the Lizard peninsula, where the church lies. The 15th-century font is of a Cornish type, but with the unusual feature of an inscription recording the name of the rector at the time it was built.

The Norman south door has serpentine columns and is decorated with zigzag and circles. It is protected by a battlemented porch.

105 ALTARNUN, Cornwall. St Nonna has a tower more than 100 feet high and dominates the village below it. This fine Perpendicular church has nave piers with their capitals and bases made of single blocks of moorstone (granite). The window tracery is unusual but of a type found locally. The large Norman font is strikingly decorated with faces at the corners and rosettes between.

Perhaps, however, the most interesting feature is the large collection of bench-ends, which include a jester with cap and bells, a fiddler and a man playing the bagpipes.

The mediaeval rood-screen and the 17th-century altar-rails stretch completely across nave and aisles.

Altarnun means 'altar of Nonna' who was St David's mother.

GLOSSARY OF ARCHITECTURAL TERMS

ABACUS: Uppermost part of a capital.

AMBULATORY: Semicircular or polygonal aisle.

APSE: Semicircular or polygonal termination to chancel.

ARCADE: A series of arches, either open or closed (blind), with masonry supported by columns, piers or pillars.

ASHLAR: Hewn or squared stone.

BALL-FLOWER: Form of 14th-century decoration – globular flower with three incurved petals

BALUSTER: A small pillar usually made circular, and swelling in the middle or towards the bottom.

BASE: The lower part of a column or pillar.

BAY: A principal compartment or division in an arcade.

BELLCOTE: Timber or stone framework on roof from which to suspend bells.

BOSS: Projecting ornament, placed at the intersection of the ribs of ceilings.

BOX PEW: Pew with a high wooden enclosure.

BROACH: Half-pyramid covering base of spire.

BUTTRESS: Projection from wall to provide additional strength and support.

CAMBERED: Slightly arched.

CAMPANILE: Bell-tower, usually detached.

CAPITAL: Head of a column or pier.

CARDINAL: North, south, east and west.

CHAMFER: Angle pared off.

CHANTRY CHAPEL: A chapel endowed by the founder for the chanting of Masses for his soul or by a guild for its members.

CHAPTER HOUSE: The place of assembly for the dean and canons in a cathedral.

CHEVRON: Norman moulding in the form of a zigzag.

Abacus, *c.* 1220, Paul's Cray, Kent.

Abacus, *c.* 1480, Croydon, Surrey.

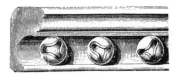
Ball-flower, Kidlington, Oxfordshire.

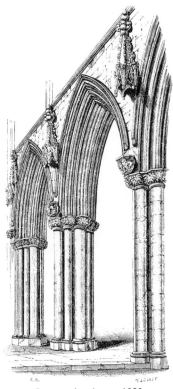
Decorated arches, *c.* 1320,
Selby Abbey, Yorkshire.

Decorated capital,
Beverley Minster, Yorkshire.

Capital, *c.* 1320,
Hampton Poyle,
Oxfordshire.

Capital, *c.* 1350,
Sandhurst, Kent.

263

CLERESTORY: Upper storey, normally of nave with row of windows.

COLLEGIATE CHURCH: Church endowed for a college of priests.

CORBEL: Stone bracket.

CORBEL TABLE: A row of corbels supporting a parapet or cornice.

COVING: Arched undersurface.

CROCKET: Leaf-shaped projection.

CROSSING: Space at the intersection of nave, chancel and transepts.

CRYPT: A vaulted space beneath a building, partly or entirely below ground.

CUPOLA: Small rounded dome raised on supports.

CUSP: Projecting point in tracery or arch.

DADO: Decoration on lower part of wall.

DOG-TOOTH: Early English decoration in form of raised stars.

DORMER: Projecting upright window in sloping roof or spire.

DRESSED STONE: Stone cut to serve as frame for walls or windows.

EASTER SEPULCHRE: Structure for holding the Sacrament just before Easter.

FAN VAULTING: See vaulting.

FENESTRATION: Window arrangement.

FILLET: Narrow, flat band running along shaft or moulding.

FLYING BUTTRESS: Buttress arched out from a wall to carry roof pressure downward and outward.

FONT CANOPY: Wooden structure completely enveloping font.

GARGOYLE: Projecting spout in human or animal shape for throwing water clear of roof.

HOOD-MOULD (Dripstone or Label): Projecting moulding above arch or window to throw off water.

IMPOST: Capital on top of pilaster or pier from which arch springs.

JAMB: Side of a doorway or window.

JESSE WINDOW: Window in which glass or stonework forms Tree of Jesse, representing genealogy of Christ.

LABEL-STOP: Ornamental head or other shape at end of hood-mould.

LADY CHAPEL: Chapel dedicated to the Virgin Mary.

LANCET: Slender pointed window.

LAY RECTOR: Layman who receives the rectorial tithes of a parish, or in whom the rectory is vested.

LIERNE VAULT: See vaulting.

LIGHT: Vertical division of window.

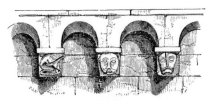

Corbel-table, St Peter's, Oxford.

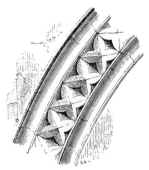

Dog-tooth, Canterbury Cathedral.

Easter Sepulchre, Stanton St John, Oxfordshire.

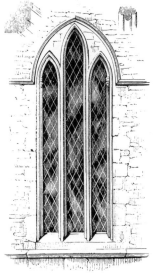

Triple lancet, *c.* 1230,
Warmington, Northamptonshire.

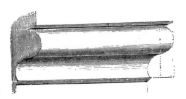

Ogee moulding

265

Jesse window, Dorchester Abbey, Oxfordshire.

LOZENGE: Diamond shape.

MOULDING: Outline given to arches, bases and capitals.

NAIL-HEAD: Late Norman decoration in form of a square raised to a centre.

NICHE: Recess in wall for statue.

NIMBUS: Halo.

OGEE: Partly concave and partly convex shape.

ORDER: Receding arch of a doorway or window.

PIER: Free-standing solid support between arches.

PILASTER: Shallow pier attached to and projecting from wall.

PILLAR: Free-standing support of arch, generally ornamental as well as structural.

PISCINA: Shallow basin with drain near altar.

PLINTH: Projecting base of column or pillar.

POPPYHEAD: Fleur-de-lis elevated termination of bench end.

PORTICUS: Side chamber.

PULPIT: Raised stage from which sermons are delivered.

PULPITUM: Stone screen shutting off the choir from the nave in a major church.

QUOIN: Dressed stone at angle.

RECTOR: Incumbent of a parish, the great tithes of which he used to retain.

REREDOS: Wall or screen behind altar, usually ornamented.

RETROCHOIR: Part of cathedral or large church behind high altar.

ROLL-MOULDING: Moulding of generally semicircular section.

ROOD: A cross or crucifix.

ROOD-LOFT: Means of access for cleaning, lighting and decking rood and sometimes acting as base for it. It also provided accommodation for choir and instrumentalists.

ROOD-SCREEN: Screen, stone or wooden, below the rood separating chancel from nave.

ROSE- or WHEEL-WINDOW: Circular window with tracery radiating from centre.

SADDLEBACK: Tower roof shaped like a timber gable.

SEDILIA: Recessed stone seats in chancel for priest and assistants.

SGRAFFITO: Design incised in plaster.

SHAFT: Small column.

SPANDREL: Triangular wall surface in the angle between two arches.

Niche, *c*. 1450, Kidlington, Oxfordshire.

Piscina, *c*. 1350, Cumnor, Berkshire.

Poppyhead, *c*. 1450,
Kidlington, Oxfordshire.

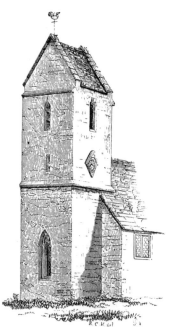

Saddleback roof, *c*. 1260, Brookthorpe, Gloucestershire.

SPIRELIGHT: Projecting opening in spire for ventilation.

STAIR-TURRET: Stone stairway giving access to tower stages.

STALL: Fixed seat, usually with carving, in choir or chancel.

STRING-COURSE: Projecting horizontal band or moulding on surface of wall.

THREE-DECKER PULPIT: Pulpit with clerk's stall and reading-desk below.

TRACERY:

(a) *Bar/Geometrical*. Form evolved at end of Early English period in which the head of a window is filled with Geometrical forms, at first simple and constructed of bars of stone but later developed into more varied shapes.

(b) *Reticulated*. Decorated form composed of ogee shapes producing net-like pattern.

(c) *Kentish tracery*. Star-like forms with spikes.

(d) *Flowing*. Later Decorated forms in which circular and ogee shapes are eliminated.

(e) *Perpendicular*. Rectilinear form in which vertical bars (mullions) carry right up into head of window.

TRANSEPT: Transverse portion of a cruciform church.

TRANSOM: Horizontal window bar.

TRIBUNE: Storey above aisle with arched openings to nave.

TYMPANUM: Space in head of doorway arch.

VAULT: Arched roof of stone.

(a) *Fan-vault*. A type of vault in which the length and curvature of the ribs, which spring from the same point, are similar.

(b) *Lierne-vault*. A vault incorporating decorative short, subsidiary ribs (liernes).

(c) *Rib-vault*. A vault with ribs projecting along the groin.

VICAR: Incumbent of a parish, the great tithes of which did not belong to him.

WHEEL-WINDOW: See rose-window.

Transom, Headcorn, Kent.

Sedilia, Lenham, Kent.

Fan-vaulting.

Vault, *c.* 1260, Westminster Abbey.

BIBLIOGRAPHY

Allen, Frank J., *The Great Church Towers of England* (Cambridge University Press, 1932).

Atkinson, T. D., *Local Style in English Architecture* (Batsford, 1947).

Betjeman, Sir John, *Collins' Guide to English Parish Churches* (Collins, 1958).

Clifton-Taylor, Alec, *The Cathedrals of England* (Thames & Hudson, 1967).

Clifton-Taylor, Alec, *The Pattern of English Building* (Faber & Faber Ltd, 1972).

Cox, J. Charles and Ford, C. B., *The Parish Churches of England* (Batsford, 1935).

Crossley, F. H., *English Church Design 1040–1540* (Batsford, 1945).

Harries, John, *Discovering Stained Glass* (Shire Publications, 1968).

Howard, F. E., *Mediaeval Styles of the English Parish Church* (Batsford, 1936).

Jones, Lawrence E., *The Observer's Book of Old English Churches* (Warne, 1973).

Jones, Lawrence E., *A Guide to some Interesting Old English Churches* (Historic Churches Preservation Trust).

Moorman, Bishop John R. H., *A History of the Church in England* (A. & C. Black, 1967).

Pevsner, Sir Nikolaus, *The Buildings of England* (Penguin Books, varying).

Piper, John, *Oxfordshire – A Shell Guide* (Faber & Faber, 1938).

Stoll, Robert, *Architecture and Sculpture in Early Britain* (Thames & Hudson, 1967).

Wickham, A. K., *Churches of Somerset* (David & Charles, 1965).

INDEX

277